Parenting for College

Real Deal Strategies to Get Admitted
& Graduate Debt Free

DR. SONYA SHULER-OKOLI

Published in Atlanta, Georgia, by *Willow Tree Books.*

Books may be purchased in bulk for educational, business, fundraising, or sales promotional use. If you would like to use material from the book, prior written permission must be obtained by email to hello@drsonyaokoli.com. Thank you for supporting the author's rights.

Library of Congress Cataloging-in-Publication Data

ISBN: 978-0-578-51629-5
Library of Congress Control Number:2019909592

Credits
Editorial: Carla DuPont
Cover Design: BE Designs
Interior Design: Carla DuPont
Photography: BQ Media Group

Printed in the United States of America

Table of Contents

Introduction
Why I Wrote This Book................................*vi*

Chapter One
Team Get That Baby To College *10*

Chapter Two
Do You Speak Higher Ed *16*

Chapter Three
How To Do High School *32*

Chapter Four
Best Fit vs. Top Ranked............................*61*

Chapter Five
Early Career Exploration Advice...................*77*

Chapter Six
The Power of Summer Bridge Programs..........*100*

Chapter Seven
Beyond A College Tour............................*110*

Chapter Eight
Colleges Have Wish Lists Too......................*121*

iv

Chapter Nine
Don't Forget Plan B……………………………....131

Chapter Ten
The Financial Frontier……………………….....147

About the Author…………………………...184

Parenting for College

Real Deal Strategies to Get Admitted
& Graduate Debt Free

Introduction

Why I Wrote This Book

Greetings, I'm Dr. Sonya----The College Dr.

As America's Favorite College Planning Expert & Parent Education Coach my goal is to help minority students and their families get strategic about college! I am a former College Dean of Academics with 13+ years of professional experience, so it's pretty safe to say I've seen it all, done it all, and chose to write a darn book about it. From grade school to graduate school this girl has been around the block and back again.

At the start of my academic career in K-12 as an educational researcher focused on multicultural pedagogical practices in urban schools. I was fortunate to get some pretty good insight into the scholastic motivations of school parents. By design, I later made my way up the ladder vertically landing key higher education leadership roles from Financial Aid Counselor to College Dean of Academics.

Ironically, the inspiration for this book came after becoming professionally frustrated with the gut-wrenching feeling felt each time I met with minority families who would share the most hurtful story. One starting with, "I wish we'd heard this years ago." Thus, decided it was time for an insider to share the unobvious info, with the power to adjust trajectory and legacy for generations to come.

Here's the deal. Our world is full of opinions and "experts," folks who made it to the frontier willing to sell "quiet as kept" info. Then, there are those with promises to make all of your family's dreams come true...for a small fortune of course. Thankfully, there were no prerequisites to getting your hands on this guide filled with strategies and proven results.

I've also found, many students of color believe that if they just land at the top of their high school class ranking, get admitted and graduate from the BEST COLLEGE, snagging a high paying dream job is "guaranteed". Sadly, each year thousands leave college broke, jobless, in debt, and some without even a degree to show for it. My first fresh out of college job, came with a whopping 25K annual salary and mortgage-sized student loan payment to match. I wish I could wink twice and teleport back in time armed with 20/20 hindsight.

Now, take a second to walk with me, *Back to the Future* style, to 1994. I was a young, green, and wet behind the ears high school freshman, glued to the TV every Thursday night watching *A Different World* and dreaming of going off to a college like a Hillman. Each semester, I floated through classes, signed up for socials, turned my nose up at clubs and avoided extracurricular activities that interfered with my "me" time, all while failing to take college planning seriously.

The reality is, those jacked up happenstances were totally avoidable; but, only if my parents and I had gotten ourselves in the know earlier. So take it from someone kicking cans on an astronomical amount of student loan debt. If hindsight could pay Sallie Mae, I'd be debt free---well, kind of. Lucky for you, those poor decisions combined with a family without connection or resources, paved the way for my current passion of helping YOU connect those dots.

Look, I get it, you feel defeated and like none of this stuff will matter anyway. The rich will keep getting richer and paying their way into the illusion that they are the "BEST and Brightest." I understand how tough it is to stay encouraged especially with media headlines on title 1 school achievement gaps, the school to prison pipeline and FBI accusations #VarsityBlues college admissions cheating scandal. But guess what? Your Go-to-College Doc is here willing and ready to provide my ordinary, hard-working folks with the insider playbook.

With that said, could your family use….

- Proactive strategies on how to maneuver high school with college in mind.

- Advice on how to speak career exploration during the middle school years to ensure productivity through college.

- And the antidote to avoid crippling student loan debt.

If you answered 'Heck Yeah" to ALL, then let's do this!

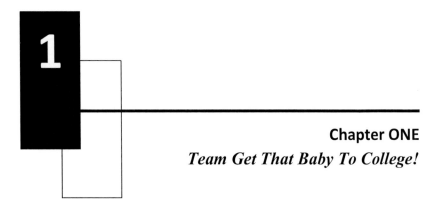

Chapter ONE
Team Get That Baby To College!

Families are not one-size-fits-all and the roles they play in a student's college planning process isn't either. However, one thing I am pretty comfortable betting my check on, is that most of the educational decisions made in your family are led by none other than mom. Guess what? In my home, that is most certainly the case, as all educational roads start and end with yours truly. For obvious reasons of course, I am an educator by profession. Also because my husband provided his full Memorandum of Understanding outlining the partnership of parenting where Mom is the 'quarter back of schooling' *ha!* No biggie, I accept the role gladly as after all we are, TEAM GET THEM BABIES TO COLLEGE!

As a professional, let me tell you I am not surprised that 8 out of 10 of my encounters with college readiness stuff are with somebody's mama.

I mean the resourceful, by-the-book, 'I eat, sleep, and breathe how to get my child ahead of the 8 ball' type of mama. On top of that, speaking engagements, conference sessions, coaching meetings all consistently booked by….you got it, Mama. To be fair, a few dads too, every once in a blue moon. Ok, but back to Mom. I've witnessed moms book academic advisement appointments, guidance counseling sessions, grab applications to summer programs, and actually sit in on meetings as a note taker while their child is doing extracurricular activities. They even field questions that their child should be asking and understanding. Because after all, the execution lies totally on them right.

Moms are totally comfortable acting as agents, which we all know quickly turns into 'I'll just do all the work then fill my child in later.' And dads are not exempt from this either. I refer to all dads as 'the closer' as if all else fails, they will be the voice of reason or write the damn check already. *HA*!

Parents, listen up. No matter the approach, this behavior is really tap dancing on a fine line of over-coddling and counterproductive to the teenager rite of passage to learn how to take care of business. Why? Well, because not only does it handicap your child's problem solving development, but may take away a level of accountability needed to manage life altering situations down the line. The goal must be to promote an environment where your child has the tools needed to take accountability and responsibility for their academics seriously. As such, you might want to allow this to be the time for things to organically unfold into a maturity-driven, beautifully orchestrated thing. Plus, let me tell you a little known secret. Sometimes parents make matters a wee bit worse by interfering with processes designed to be student initiated.

All Hands On Deck

The college setting has a slight built-in roadblock for the eager beaver type of parent, called FERPA (Family Education Rights and Privacy Act). FERPA is very similar to what HIPPA means in the medical world as it relates to records. FERPA can smack you in the face by minimizing parental access or control once a student is enrolled. Even with certain Dual Enrollment or college bridge programs, where your child is then identified as a college student, the understanding is that he/she can operate with limited takeover.

Again, instill in your child how to handle their personal journey with you overseeing rather than intervening. The backfire to being an overbearing,

24/7 helicopter parent is setting this unrealistic expectation that Mom will fix it all. Although I am a committee member of the Tiger Mom Club, LOL, I am here to say that a team approach including the entire family is best.

The college road is a process that starts well before the scouting of schools begins. There are many pit-stops and relationship building steps along the way taking place years in advance, including forming relationships with individuals who have been there, done that, and have been in your current shoes. You will find many willing to, not only share stories, but provide you with resources to help. It is a good practice to speak with those whose children are similar to where your child is academically and often geographically. I remember meeting a mom-dad duo who were conducting small group sessions through a youth ministry at their church. It was nothing formal or staged, just impromptu conversations about things they'd learned, roads they took, and how they worked the system from kindergarten to college to ensure their daughter attended a competitive school.

The thing I loved about their story was how they literally tag teamed it. Mom was the one burning the midnight oil on the internet finding out school choice stuff, programs, summer camps, and academic enrichment stuff, while dad worked the extracurricular circuit speaking with coaches and other parents on stuff that was a must when sports was a back-up plan. Together, each worked with their daughter on a different aspect and provided her with a balanced view of the steps she needed to take and when.

In the end, when it was time for their child to make her final decision, she was faced with many options, reflective of institutions she actually wanted to attend because they were a good fit.

I know every family looks forward to the day their hard work pays off. Many have huddled on the field for each and every decision from daycare to college decision day. After all, our nation's schooling process is built on a parental involvement model for a reason. I guarantee that if you just say these words to any teacher, principal or guidance counselor, they would respond with a praise dance. *Ha!* Then, immediately share how much more valuable and rewarding the journey is for students when the parental partnership is ignited and on fire. You must understand the importance of on-field huddles sooner than later. For some, this happens the minute they're taking those first day of school pictures. For others, this may not begin until their child begins showing true interest in college. Regardless of how you do it, just make sure it is done... sooner than later.

Word to the wise, *the most academically prepared student is one with the most resourceful family of cheerleaders rallying behind them.*

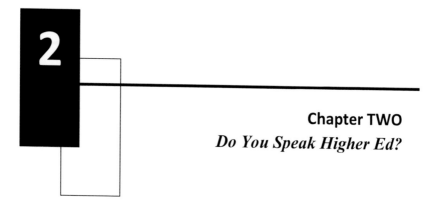

Chapter TWO

Do You Speak Higher Ed?

The American higher education system is a hierarchy with multiple levels. Each level builds upon the one before. As you probably already know, a hierarchy is a system in which groups are ranked one above the other according to status or authority. Colleges and universities are made up of several types of institutional profiles with unique credentials. As such, one who is interested in pursuing studies beyond high school must first understand that the very next level is called, higher education. Now, before you pass go or collect their $200, it is time to become familiar with said levels, then determine which will promote the reaching of personal or professional goals.

Education Beyond High School

For reasons of simplicity we will only highlight the traditional levels. Of course we could probably add a few depending on occupation or career goals.

According to the Department of Education, here are the basic levels:

1. Certificate/Diploma
2. Associate
3. Bachelor's
4. Master's
5. Doctorate

The Certificate/Diploma Level

When looking to determine the difference between educational tracks, it typically all boils down to the length of time it takes to complete. To ensure we are all working with functional and relevant definitions, I will go through and briefly highlight each level. First up, certificate or diploma. As the earliest entry point, the differences between a diploma, certificate, and associate degree confuse people the most. Probably because you can pursue a diploma track that requires 6 months or so and you can also enter into a certificate track that requires 18 months to a year. Or the associate degree track, which is a standard two years in length.

So I'm sure you can see how folks like to run the three of these together. Of course, I would not be doing my job if I did not break things down just a little bit further. Diplomas require classes or training relating directly to a specific area of study, for example, Medical Office Assistant. Certificate programs often take months instead of years and some can even be obtained in conjunction with a degree program. Diploma programs offer a more in-depth curriculum than a certificate and they're often awarded through technical colleges and hospitals with specialty programs that provide training. In comparison, certificates are more compressed allowing students to effectively learn a skill without the need of core or general education coursework. A perfect example of a certificate program with training is obtaining a Paralegal Certificate.

With the paralegal program, one solely learns how to do this line of work and what it entails day-to-day. Through this level of training, you are fully skilled to go directly into the profession. Although either route leads into an entry level career, the certificate offers both a more specialized approach and skillset adaptation. The curriculum of the diploma or certificate program largely depends on the field being studied and most won't require the completion of general education coursework, like English 1101 or College Algebra.

The Associate's Degree Level

Have you ever seen a job posting that read "college preferred but not required?" Or have you ever checked out occupational postings and noticed how many have the word "assistant" at the end, like Physical Therapy Assistant, Teaching Assistant, or Nursing Assistant?

Well, guess what? These folks are the lovely recipients of a two-year associate's degree. Often praised for the affordability, limited time to completion, and hands-on real world classroom application, this has been the go-to-degree for students looking for less, but meaningful career options.

In our world, an associate degree basically translates into the first two years of a bachelor's degree (freshman/sophomore year).

Types of Associate's Degrees:
- Associate of Arts (AA)
- Associate of Science (AS)
- Associate of Applied Science (AAS)

In looking at the three types of associate degrees, you may be asking yourself what the differences are. Simply put, the difference is the rigorous nature of the courses a student must take.

Think about it like this, AAs focus on the liberal arts and the AS, math and science. They prepare students who desire a bachelor's level education upon completion. The AAS is focused in applied sciences, implying courses are more practical/general to prepare students for career or vocation.

Overall, this level is a foundational degree collaboratively built on general education coursework from the areas of social sciences, arts, mathematics, English, and science. This proves just why it is the consistent student choice award winner for being a universally good fit. From the adult going back to college after being out of school for some time to the high schooler just trying to get his/her feet wet, this option can be good. With this, it is no secret as to why many use it as a launching pad to go on to earn their bachelor's degree a few years later. I personally adore this level as it really does offer students the best trial run for determining if college is the right move or to test the aptitude of whether or not they will cut the mustard for university.

The Bachelor's Degree Level

A bachelor's degree is totally undebated as one of the most commonly recognized levels of higher education. I literally preach to anyone who will listen about earning the greatest equalizer.

I believe this is due to the fact that it's internationally known which, in essence, gives anyone who is brave enough to tough the tumultuous waters to attain it a universal nod that they have what it takes to see a task through to completion.

What are the types of bachelor's degrees?

Bachelor of Arts (B.A.)

This degree typically requires a broad variety of coursework in humanities, social sciences, arts, or music.

Bachelor of Science (B.S.)

This degree typically requires specialized coursework specific to one's desired major, typically courses in science and math.

Bachelor of Fine Arts (BFA)

This degree usually entails a creative or artistic focus with coursework in art related disciplines.

Bachelor of Applied Science (BAS)

This degree requires specialized coursework specific to unconventional business majors like supply chain and logistics. Those interested should already have an Associate of Applied Science and related work experience.

Alright, now let's break down the BAS even further. This one gets pretty sticky because many feel that it generally kind of sets students up for a lack of options. While others strongly feel it is just a watered-down degree for those with limited options due to academic aptitude. Like I said earlier, "applied" implies practical and real-world. SO, pursue with caution.

Overall, the bachelor degree is the standard educational credential for those looking to land "professional" level employment. The BA/BS degree is typically the entry level ticket to the most common career paths in the U.S. workforce.

The Master's Degree Level

The next level, master's degree, is where one goes from an undergraduate to a graduate student. As the step immediately following the obtainment of a bachelor's degree, the next degree that can be earned is called a graduate degree. Some universities offer it as an additional leg to the bachelor's program, where course work is extended another year and a half or so.

To explain further, the master's degree is an academically rigorous level of study focused on a specialty career area within one's major or discipline. Folks often get a master's degree in the same major as their bachelor's.

As a matter of practice, it is often best to do just that versus picking up an entirely new area of study that you know nothing about or, should I say, have extremely limited knowledge in as you only took a few courses of it in college. Those who pursue a master's degree typically have a desire to climb high on the career ladder and reach the glass ceiling. Or they want to be recognized as having honed their craft to the level of expertise needed to be considered highly qualified versus just knowledgeable on the subject.

Other than the length of time, admission criteria, and standards for program entry, the degree differs in the final year of studies. With this, on top of the standard comprehensive exam, one must also construct either a research paper, culmination capstone project, or thesis.

Types of Master's Degrees:

Wow, there are just too doggone many to list. So I will just note a few of the most popular:

- MBA - Master of Business Administration
- MSW - Master of Social Work
- MAC - Master of Accountancy

- M.Ed - Master of Education

The Doctoral Degree

Alrighty now! Last but certainly not least...not in spirit, nor in truth. *Ha!* This is the big kahuna, the fat lady singing, the end of the journey, and affectionately known as, "**PH**inally **D**one well if ya getting a Ph.D." Sorry, I got off on a tangent, but what I am trying to say is that this is the last level of the American higher education system.

This level is totally occupationally oriented given students determine this level of schooling solely based on their career objective; ultimately where they see themselves going into retirement. I mean hey, it ain't referred to as a terminal degree for nothing. Seriously, because folks don't embark on this long journey without career plans of longevity. Now while the doctoral degree seems so far off the college prep topic boat, just know that it is extremely important to engage in some thought about it during planning.

With respect to the doctoral degree process, that could totally be a book all on its own. I am simply saying that knowing your end game, be that law school, medical school, or attaining a Ph.D., can shape your undergraduate college decision making process.

Terminal Degrees Are Needed for Careers In:
- Pharmacist
- Dentist
- Professor
- Medical Doctor
- Physical Therapist
- Attorney

College vs. University, Do You Know The Difference?

So now that you got a test drive on what the higher education system looks like, there is just one small little thing I need to know, "Do you know the difference between a college and university?"

Well, let me tell you, during my speaking engagements, this is one of my opening questions. Parents and students begin looking around the room as if I'm telling a joke every time I ask this question. Some even laugh out loud with looks on their faces like, *Duh! Obviously you're not serious*. Then moments after the imaginary Jeopardy song plays, I get folks who suddenly realize they have no clue.

Ironically, many folks don't know this difference, even those who have attended one or the other. However, knowing this very distinct difference is something that should be at the top of every family's list while on the road to Destination College. Why? Because at the delineation between a college and a university are important characteristics that will make or break your child's experience or expectations. Here is the skinny on it. While college and university are often used interchangeably, they are not the same thing.

Yes, both are institutions of higher education. Yes, both provide students bachelor's degrees upon graduation. However, the interworking/intricacies of the academic offerings presented in each are vastly different. For example, colleges are usually smaller and streamlined with the bachelor's degree representing the highest awarded degree. On the other hand, universities are larger in size, with majors of study within "schools" and those schools are referred to as colleges. For example, at Georgia State University, the Business major is housed inside The Rollins School of Business. Subsequently, at Howard University, Journalism is housed within the Cathy Hughes School of Communications.

Let's check out a few descriptors related to this topic:
The Institutional Types:
Research Institution
Comprehensive
Ivy League
Highly Selective

Now I'll cover just the first one, R1/Research One and R2/Research Two Institutions as they are most widely known probably because they're normally your "State University of" which typically offers high scholastic achievement and research opportunities for undergraduate students. Here, students can take core courses as freshman and sophomores, then apply them to a major. Declaring a major is a separate application process occurring after one has been accepted into the institution. The process may include additional testing requirements, review of college coursework and even recommendation letters from faculty/staff. On the other hand, colleges have a much smaller population of students with fewer majors and students select a major at any time without an actual admission process into a "school of".

Institutional Characteristics/Descriptors:
Historically Black College/University (HBCU)
Hispanic Serving Institution (HIS)
Public School
Private School
For Profit/Non Profit

Why Is Knowing Differences Important?

Prospective college students must understand the intricacies of higher education because this will save time, energy, money, and heartache. Ultimately, being able to delineate between college and university can help avoid enrolling somewhere not in alignment with your goals.

As getting a head start is important, it is also important to get our thoughts in order so building that College Wish List doesn't seem like a chore. The College Wish List, represents a list of ideals and expectations that will make the upcoming 4 to 5 years as seamless as possible.

Here are a few example questions to think about while drafting that list:

- What is the optimal classroom environment where I thrive?
- Do I perform better with larger or smaller class sizes?
- Do I enjoy diversity and building relationships with those who may not look like me or those who may not share my cultural beliefs and practices?
- How do I feel when people do not know me or even my first or last name?
- What type of instructional experience do I expect to be challenged by?

Think about higher education institutions in your town, find one college and one university. Now grab your phone and do a quick Google search to determine:

- Total student population
- Number of degree programs
- Interesting Fact/Ranking

For example, my local university, Georgia State reports 51,000 students, along with over 250 degree programs offered and is the #2 Most Innovative University in the country, Pretty AWESOME right!? So how many students do you think would sit inside of those lectures with me? Let me help you; I could probably expect about 150 classmates. Now would this be terribly intimidating for your kid? These are the types of questions to think about.

Alright, so far you have been given a wealth of background information about the makeup of colleges and universities. I feel college stuff is like one of those topics folks feel doesn't require much thought. Possibly because it's such an ordinary topic of conversation that we just chalk it up to something we have a pretty good level of understanding about.

What many of us find when it's show time, is that just because we were great conversationalists didn't necessarily translate into understanding *thangs* for real, for real. And as a big purchase item, it is very important for any parent, future student, or supportive friend to get in the know and gather resources that will allow informed decisions to be made.

I guarantee you will avoid all of the pitfalls that lie ahead if you truly get to the root of misinformation which is often a lack of contextually relevant information. For example, if your child wants to be a paralegal and not a lawyer, she needs to know how that program will probably NOT be offered at the university level, but at a technical college. Your son needs to know that if he wants to be a physical therapy assistant, instead of looking at graduate degree options, the associate's degree level is most appropriate. Now, look at how fast I just saved your family over $100K....just like that!

All and all, I cannot stress enough how thinking about these things can never occur too early in your child's educational journey. Plowing through the details doesn't have to be the goal in doing so. Ensuring that you and your family have an in-depth understanding of your child's hopes, desires, and future expectations is needed.

As in order to create a strategic plan to guarantee these things have a chance of materializing. First things first, let's get through high school with a fool-proof strategy!

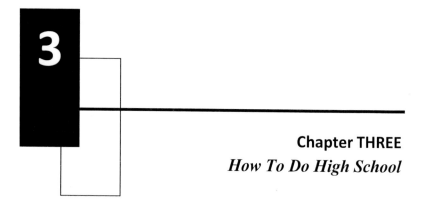

Chapter THREE

How To Do High School

Now let's talk about high school, AKA the period of time when parents lose their heads to make sure their children are in the best school district. Also universally known to be the only place where exceptional matriculation is certain to occur. Why? Well didn't you hear, top districts have been etched in stone and proven to be the ONLY way a student gets into a top college? Yeah — totally my sarcastic tone, *ha*!

While it may seem every parents' number one goal is to send their child(ren) to the best everything in the world, truth is, many just want an option with a high probability of success in nourishing a well-rounded student. In my last book, *Mom's Guide to Schooling*, I shared the ABC's of navigating the American School System; a system that can be extremely confusing even before adding stuff like school choice, types of schools, and public versus private. I often hear parents of high school students complain about how much they still don't know. Many want to be proactive so their baby will swim, not sink. Yet, too many parents start beating themselves up, or listening to those "we got it all together" parents who make them feel like they should just throw in the towel because it's too late. You know they say things like "if at this point you're still unaware of how things work, you can't possibly get ahead of a game that's almost over." Now let me be honest, yes the high school years are the tail end of proactivity, and in my professional opinion this game starts somewhere around those early school years. BUT like all things in life, you can't rule nothing you haven't tried out. So let's GET IT!

If you're the parent who has gone through school, without one piece of information about college that catches your attention until the junior/senior "college night" program, no worries, I am here for you now. Although not totally wrong, many parents take the school's lead on how to navigate this college prep process, instead of collaborating with the school guidance team to determine what's best for their child (early). So for those of you who are not quite raising a high schooler just yet...I'm warning you now, college planning must start as early as elementary, middle school at the very latest.

So since we are talking about "early" grades and being proactive. Here is a quick tip: "Focus on is an elevated level of collaboration with your child's teachers to reinforce the belief in his/her ability to meet/surpass scholastic benchmarks."

A student who believes very highly in their potential often does better than one who doesn't. Think about math for example. Those who think, *I'm terrible at math* often always fall to the bottom of the pack because of this negative connotation. Because of this, some may have experienced teachers who let them soak in that belief.

Let's face it, even with our own children it is hard to motivate a child who doesn't think they can do it, let alone be responsible in a classroom with 22 other children present. Yet there are tons of stellar teachers who can motivate and do it well daily. But as parents, our job is to reiterate this same support at home by re-routing our child's negative self-talk. As a student who struggled with math, I can relate. Not only did I hate it, but I just didn't get it and there was nothing anyone could say to help me see it any other way. As an adult, I am the master deflector of all things math and avoid it like the plague. Lucky for my children, I married a man who absolutely loves it!

Any who, with all that said, I am simply implying that we set the academic stage at home, so our children embrace concepts with familiarity when at school.

So how soon should we begin setting the stage? Some think preschool is too early and others think middle school is too late. My advice is follow your child's lead. As soon as he/she begins talking academics or shows concerns with actual grades, it's time. In my experience most do so around 2rd grade. Probably due to the fact that many begin reading like a big kid around this time. Anyway, truth is, even if you by-pass elementary, you are still in luck as middle school is not too late to lay the groundwork in establishing that solid academic foundation. As such, your child will be ready to hit the ground running right on into the rigorous high school coursework coming soon!

Speaking of H.S. Coursework

Once enrolled in high school, the expectation is that your child will have the option of advancing through various curriculum tracks such as:

- Advanced Placement (AP)
- College Prep (CP)
- Dual Enrollment (DE)
- Honors

- International Baccalaureate (IB)

High school curriculum tracks are very important as colleges look at the "most" academically rigorous coursework in determining your child's aptitude for success in college. Therefore, it is important that the foundation is set early enough so when they do get to high school, they jump right into one of these tracks, with clarity on the option where the best possible grades can be earned. In order to identify the best track, you must know your child's strengths and areas of opportunity.

High School Strategy

Let's talk about another must know in the realm of high school strategy. The thing about high school academics is, everything is categorized by high performers and low performers. A third category is, "at risk." This is otherwise known as we need to take proper precautions to ensure failure of courses or worse doesn't occur.

At this part of the journey, it's important to know where you're going and how you *plan* to get there. Let's say Princeton is on the list...then you need to know their selection criteria the minute the thought crosses your mind, or Howard University, same logic applies. Basically, your child must matriculate through high school mirroring what you all have read are things the admissions officers may look for in a prospective student.

Here are the a few things you all want to determine:

1. **What is the selection criteria?**

   Does the admissions review appear to weigh grades, GPA, letters of recommendation in a specific manner, OR does the college not give any specifics? Also, note you will want to review the previous year's freshman class profile. This is typically available for public consumption as it will allow you all to get a feel for the way the school sways.

2. **Which test, ACT or SAT, is mentioned most?**

   Many colleges say that they'll take either, however look for cues to let you in on if one is favored over the other.

3. **Does the admissions page discuss High School Curriculum Tracks (AP/College Prep/IB)?**

   Rule of thumb: colleges are always concerned with what type and level of coursework students pursued. This is due to the fact that the academic rigor is often linked to aptitude to succeed at the college level.

When thinking about High School Curriculum Tracks, I want you to also note how colleges look at a student's high school individually. They go out of their way to really get to know what's going down academically at that school. With regard to rigor, what's considered the most academically rigorous is simply the highest track available at that high school. Thus, if your child's high school only offers college prep, then this is the most academically rigorous track available. No worries, then, if you don't have the AP schedule the college you're scouting appears to desire. Good news is, you won't be ruled out. Check out the University of California's admissions team reference to this on their webpage:

"We consider class rank (if available) and the rigor of your curriculum, including the number of advanced courses taken (if offered by your school)."

In addition, to rigor another key point of importance is the infamous Grade Point Average (GPA). In my opinion, GPA represents the foundation of the academic house. The higher it is, the higher the odds of a sturdy home being built. Subsequently

what's needed to build this college bound home
includes:

- Extracurricular Activities
- Community Engagement & Volunteer
  Experiences
- Persuasive Writing
- Participation in Bridge Programs
- Academically Rigorous Curriculum Tracks
  (Honors, AP, IB, and sometimes Dual
  Enrollment)

While each item above is important to building that solid college application, the most important variable is simply, what college are you trying to get admitted to? Because the type of institution your child is hoping to get into will give a pretty good idea of those items the admissions committee will be looking for your baby to have on lock. Highly Selective/Ivy Leagues will most certainly consider the most academically rigorous track as one of the variables at the very top on their list of must haves followed by GPA. Again, please ensure you all first determine the curriculum tracks available at your school, then work with a guidance counselor to determine the most suitable for your child and where he/she is headed to for college.

Let's Talk High School Curriculum Tracks

High school curriculum tracks are of super importance for parents and students. Each semester, when it's time to create that class schedule, you all need to think strategically about those academic end goals. You must also be realistic and practical about the academic aptitude of your child. Not just can he/she handle the work, but do they want or have time to pump out good grades when adding in things like basketball, drama club, and part-time employment.

I've witnessed parents get all up in a roar demanding their child take the hardest classes known to man because of their goal to get into the BEST college. Honestly, I cringe a bit when hearing this because sometimes having students take the hardest class and getting a bad grade, harms more than it helps. When parents have this fixed mindset, they don't realize it might be better to encourage classes their child is comfortable with even if those are not the "hardest" classes. The reality is, there is more than one way top institutions consider student applications competitive.

Therefore, if your child will pursue at least one of the academically rigorous tracks available Advanced

Placement, International Baccalaureate and High School Honors, they have a shot.

Advanced Placement (AP)

Let's start with AP, AKA, a whole can of worms if not fully understood. I say this because not grasping the intricacies of how the program works in high school can pose college acceptance challenges.

AP was created by the College Board as an opportunity for students to pursue college-level work for credit and placement while matriculating high school. At the completion of the course(s) students must pass the AP exam. A passing score provides credit and placement. Placement refers to being placed in a position to "skip" the general education core classes usually required during the first years of college. Therefore, a passing grade and score on the AP English exam, awards the student ENG 101 college credit along with H.S. English credit. But a non-favorable mark will receive H.S. credit only.

Tons of parents think the aim must be to take ALL of the AP classes offered. I must caution you against this and here's why. Upon successfully completing an AP course, you are required to take an exam very similar to that of a standardized test. The results determine if credit will be given. If your child does not do well on the AP exam, the course won't count for college credit. With this, the earned grade is then only factored into the high school GPA and graduation credits.

In a situation like this, your child may feel defeated given she devoted a considerable amount of time, effort, and energy that she probably could have utilized on a less rigorous course, like College Prep (CP) and aced it. And while I believe strongly that ANY student seeking to get into a reputable university should take at least one AP course, like English for example, I am not an advocate of a student just taking all rigorous classes just for the heck of it. Guess what, that ain't strategy. This can actually shoot your baby in the foot. A more strategically practical approach would be to consider rigorous coursework as a way to "better" position your child for college. Hence, a better strategy would be to select AP coursework in subjects where solid grades are consistently earned. For example, NOT letting them take AP Chemistry when you know they are getting C's in the general/standard level Chemistry course because the likelihood of them passing the AP course let alone the examination, is slim.

From professional experience let me tell you, most colleges prefer a diverse mix of courses to compliment a respectable GPA and SAT/ACT score. Now you link all that to a compelling major representing your interest and boom goes the dynamite! Let me explain this more, IF your child is a rock star at language arts, consider AP Language and Composition. But if your child is a little iffy in history you might not want them to register for AP U.S. World History.

International Baccalaureate (IB)

Now let me pause here to chat just a little about International Baccalaureate or the (IB) track. IB is an international credential program with goals of preparing students for success in life and college. It is designed to shape students' intellectual, social, emotional, and physical well-being, along with critical thinking. Equipped with options to take either a few courses or pursue the prestigious IB diploma, which includes six subject groups. Although students describe the diploma track as daunting, those willing to pursue it totally position themselves for the possibility of saving a years' worth of college work. How, you ask? Well a few institutions waive their general education/core class requirement in lieu of the IB Diploma.

For example, check out the University of Utah's admissions website which states the following: *General education requirements will be waived for completion of the IB Diploma except in the areas of writing, American history, and mathematics.* Wow---how is that for tuition savings!

With IB, I will tread a little lightly, not because it's insignificant, but since it's by far the least used across high schools. This is unfortunate because it's such an outstanding program.

The main reason many high schools don't offer the IB program, is because schools must invest tons of time, energy, effort, and money to receive designation as an IB school. Any way I could go on and on about that—moving on. *Ha!*

Another interesting fact, the International Baccalaureate (IB) program is not just for students here in the United States, but those interested in attending colleges around the globe can also give it a spin. In my opinion, the beautiful thing about IB is the flexibility. A student can take either just a few courses here and there, or pursue an actual diploma. The decision would largely depend on where he/she plans to attend college and how much time/energy they are willing to invest. Lastly like AP, the course completion of IB culminates with a required standardized exam in order for college credit to be awarded.

Ok let me rewind on back to this IB diploma thing. Because it is everything to me! Now let me tell you in advance, most high school students give a big ol' hard roll on this one as all they can see is a ton of work ahead of them. *HA!* Now, although getting the IB diploma is not mandatory or even required, doing so can set your baby up for a first year of college cake walk! Talk about strategy honey! Well, this would be along the lines of when strategy met smarty pants and delivered a bundle of brilliance! I mean, think about it. General education (core) classes typically makes up a significant amount, about half to be exact, of the bachelor's degree. Now wouldn't it be super-amazing if your child could totally skip a bunch of those classes and just jump right on into major courses. *WHOA!* You want to talk about savings... You guys will not only save tuition money, but possibly shave matriculation time in half. My God, how amazing would it be to complete that college degree in *record* time!

The moral of this story: if your high school offers the IB track, do yourself a favor and consider it. I would say it is totally worth making an urgent appointment at your guidance counselor's office to get the *real deal*. Oh and can you tell I am a fanatic of this option all the way baby!

High School Honors Track

We just went through key points about the Advanced Placement (AP) & International Baccalaureate (IB) tracks, now let's get into some tidbits about the High School Honors track. Given the track is not nationally credentialed, there is no standardized exam to determine placement, thus students only earn high school credit. Finally, unlike AP where the College Board decides the curriculum, Honors is overseen by local school districts, teachers, curriculum heads, or principals. Yet many parents and students think AP and Honors are interchangeable or one in and of the same. You can see, this could not be further from the truth. However, a similarity is Honors eligibility which, like the others, is based on above average academic standing. Let me pause here, because I think I failed to mention that with each track, approval to pursue will most likely come from your High School Guidance Counselor. As such, you all won't necessarily determine what you can/cannot register for. Sorry guys, you have to respect whatever process is in place at your school.

Lastly, students on the Honors track potentially earn additional GPA points calculated to increase their GPA standing.

Advance Placement vs. Honors

Families often scratch their heads to determine if they should be Team AP or Honors. First things first, AP will provide the opportunity to truly complete assignments like those in a university classroom. As a matter of practice, the syllabus often mirrors the learning objectives of the college course it represents. For example, AP Psychology will have the same student learning objectives as Intro to Psychology 101.

Another point, the student who passed the AP Exam for AP Language Arts now has a college transcript notation for ENG 101 and jumps right into ENG 102.

See, that's one less class and a few less dollars on that tuition check. Think about what we discussed earlier, rigor. From the perspective of a college admissions committee, they know the playing field was leveled given H.S. students around the country must all take the same AP exam. As AP is the "hardest" track you can conclude, AP versus Honors in their minds equates to a student who braved the MOST academically rigorous coursework available at their high school.

The moral of the story: If you want the biggest bang for your child's time, effort, and energy, and your money, AP is it hands down!

Dr. Sonya's Golden Nugget

If your child is exceeding their academic goals, yet apprehensive to take the "hardest" track. Consider stepping up just one level first. If he/she is in College Prep, then look one level up, to Honors. Then when homeruns are hit in Honors, consider one more level up to Advanced Placement (AP).

How Dual Enrollment Weighs In

Dual Enrollment structurally, may differ a bit from state to state or even within school districts. However, the premise remains the same, an opportunity for high school students to take college coursework alongside their traditional high school classes. For some schools, those college courses are offered at local colleges while others are right there at the high school or even online. Although most parents believe this is the best way to test the college readiness waters, academics are split on a number things. Many educational experts question: equity of academic rigor and is it a reasonable commitment for the average high school student to handle.

Okay a little moment of transparency here, I sit on the Dual Enrollment (DE) fence. Well kind of. Don't get me wrong, I strongly believe DE is a good way to test the waters. However, in my opinion high school is a rite of passage that students need to experience "as is."

As one living in the world of academia, I see how difficult the college world is for the traditional freshman student. I've witnessed how difficult of a time DE students have on our campuses, enrolled in high school and college at the same time. Many appear to be drowning with the level of work, faculty expectations, and overall adjustment to less hands-on instructional delivery. While, I totally find it beneficial for students to get their feet wet by possibly taking a few college level courses; but, certainly not a full-fledged degree program requiring an in-depth level of commitment for a full year or two.

Why, do I feel so strongly about this? Well, because I've encountered too many students who don't really understand what this all means for them academically. Yeah, they get the 'I will look like a rose on my college application when my dream university sees this A earned in Political Science.' But what they don't understand is that IF they make a not-so-good mark or even worse an F, this can be detrimental to their future. Too many only see this as a trial run that doesn't matter much and IF things don't go as planned no harm, no foul. The truth is, taking a course, no matter whether the outcome is good, bad, or indifferent most certainly counts!

When I was at a small community college, I witnessed students thinking they could just wish the C's away. Others solicited parents to beg it away and some who felt just giving up mid-way would do the trick. None of them realized that whatever grade you earn in that college class counts TWICE: once on your college transcript and the other on your high school transcript.

The other alarming fact, depending on your school district policies, a withdrawal or "W" grade can even become an "F" on your high school transcript since you technically did not complete the course. Now there is no way we can go down the line right now to determine the rules in each state. But for the sake of this conversation, whether your child plans to fail or withdraw, it will be visibly noticeable for prospective colleges to see. Keeping this point, another concern is your ability to graduate from high school. Subsequently, given the fact that this DE thing is a big game of credits on both sides of the coin. Please do not pass go or collect $200 until you all touch and agree with the guidance counselor, that you have sufficient credits and the course(s) in question isn't a graduation requirement. Because, if so, you're going to need to replace or make it up no matter which course of action is decided.

While I totally understand many parents want this trial run, I need you to understand how this can sometimes bite that baby in the butt! I am choosing to use my words carefully here. Yet, this is key if you have a child considered a middle performer. Although, many programs have a GPA criteria students must meet, it varies. One might start at 3.0 or higher and unfortunately others just a 2.0. My sentiment is, there is no way a student with a 2.0 is "college ready" on top of the fact that it takes more effort to be enrolled in both high school and college. Therefore you all may want to reconsider a big dive into Dual Enrollment (DE).

Switching gears to "college selection" it is important to note some admissions committees consider where your child took their Dual Enrollment college coursework. A word of advice, the institution where your child decides to do their DE courses should be a place you would be open to them attending. Thus at the end of the day, weigh all options and consider each variable as it relates to your child's academic aptitude. Please refrain from suggesting that they take college courses when you know deep-down they aren't ready. Because when they begin to submit transcripts to colleges, and let's just say they have an unsuccessful attempt, you certainly don't want them showing their bad hand up front (winks). Think about it like a card game, nobody should know what's in your hand until you decide to reveal your cards. Thus that baby shouldn't be revealing a bad hand if they don't have to.

Moral of the story: Consider alternative options or let your so-so/midlevel academic performer continue their regularly scheduled program. The flip side of this are the parents of high academic achievers. Your child is making all A's and ready to take things to the next level.

For many parents, this is the time to pull the trigger on signing them up at your local college for Dual Enrollment. But let me STOP you in those tracks. The best strategy to take with your high-achiever would be Advanced Placement (AP) or International Baccalaureate (IB) classes INSTEAD of Dual Enrollment. Ironically, some students believe Dual Enrollment provides leverage, shows an institution they can successfully handle college-level coursework. However, the fact is, admissions committees at top institutions would much rather see your child securing AP/IB over Dual Enrollment or a mix of both.

The reason is, and many won't probably ever say this directly but, DE is often seen as inferior in rigor to AP/IB because it's not viewed as a predictable measure of academic aptitude mainly because students are attending various types and ranks of colleges. Plus there is no standardization of what the outcomes are. Think about the student taking a U.S. History DE class at Yale and another at DeVry, are they created equally? Subjectivity at its finest right. However, as AP/IB are nationally recognized and have a universal curriculum where each student must sit for a nationally required standardized exam—the logic is, students are on same playing field no matter where they took DE courses. Thus the reason AP/IB weighs a wee-bit heavier on the admissions radar.

Subsequently, some colleges take DE courses into account while others flat out say (directly or indirectly), "Taking DE credits are nice, but we're only taking your actual high school coursework into account." At other institutions, upon applying, a student may feel they are being penalized for having too many college credits because over loading up those DE credits. Keep in mind, there is a credit hour threshold to be considered a traditional freshman. Depending on the academic end goal entering college as an upperclassmen is wonderful. In other cases this is not what you want, given institutions award full ride scholarships to First Year Traditional students. Thus, in this instance, although the student managed to knock out a significant amount of credits earning their rightful place as a "sophomore" or even "junior", it could disqualify them for admission or scholarships. Again, be strategic! If the strategy is to save your family tons of money by knocking out those general education (core) courses then great tactic. But in the same breath this could be detrimental--IF your child's dream school views this route unfavorably.

The Dual Enrollment Debate

In the state where I reside (Georgia) Dual

Enrollment (DE) is a program providing H.S. students an opportunity to take college coursework while enrolled in high school student. Each state may refer to it with different terminology, but the premise is the same. In the great state of Georgia, Higher Education partners offer courses at traditional college campuses, on high school grounds and even online. Although DE is a great program to get students a little college test drive; many students don't really understand what they are getting themselves into. And parents, are often confused or unaware of the pros/cons. Here is a list of items often debated about Dual Enrollment, you decide if it's a pro or con:

- Most colleges already have a High School Bridge program for local schools and offer some concessions for those who participate
- High school students in both 9th and 10th grade are welcome to sign up for DE courses
- High scholastic achievers of color are often steered into DE and away from AP & IB
- Students with GPA of 2.5 are also allowed to enroll in DE coursework
- High School class ranking often allow quality points for those who've taken DE coursework

Ironically each of the items listed are debated around the U.S. not just from the desk of Dr. Sonya D.E opponent LOL. One thing that those of us in academia hear often from admissions counselors is how they wish states would do a better job monitoring/auditing the DE program or make a case for usefulness long term.

One thing I remember vividly from my College Dean days was the number of parents who called and flooded my email during high school registration to request "solicited" advice about which track would get them into the "Best" college. Of course you all know I don't subscribe to that notion of "Best" in that manner. Yet, what I did advise was simple, AP and IB over everything, and sometimes honors. Because here's what you might NOT know:

- Highly Selective & Top Tier Colleges prefer Advanced Placement/International Baccalaureate
- You should NOT complete a full "Associate Degree" unless occupational, otherwise it is a waste of time
- Too many college credits can jeopardize the "Freshman Profile"
- An institution may push students to apply with transfer student status

- Courses at a Four Year Institution vs. a Two Year Institution are strongly preferred
- A School District's Withdraw policy may flip "W" to a grade of "F" for non-completion of an attempted class
- ONLY take courses at colleges with a respectable academic reputation avoid For-Profit or Technical Colleges
- Grades earned are indefinite and become part of a student's college transcript FOREVER

As you can see, (DE) is not one size fits all nor the cure all. Don't get me wrong there are plenty of institutions acknowledging it with open arms, accepting tons of previous credits, welcoming advanced standing and weighing applicant materials. There are just as many who secretly toss their noses up at it. And because of the inconsistency in receptiveness, you had better think twice about it!

Morale of this story, make curriculum decisions based on your academic end goals. Your decision must boil down to where you plan to attend college in the future. No matter the options you think you have, talk with your high school guidance counselor FIRST. Then make sure to engage with someone at the institution who understands the academic discipline or future major. In the end consider both sources to determine the most beneficial route to achieving those education and career end goal.

Let's Talk SAT/ACT & When Should You Begin The Prep?

I get this question all the time from parents and my answer often shocks them. Ironically unlike everything else we've discussed, this is the one area where I do not recommend doing it as early in the journey as possible. Many academic professionals strongly suggest SAT/ACT prep begin around the sophomore year of high school. The SAT/ACT of yesteryear took an antiquated approach to testing for how intelligent one was versus the transferable level of knowledge to predict college success. Whereas the new coming of age test incorporates tons of real-world, current affairs types of questions linked to the courses students typically take later in the high school journey. A big ol' high stakes game of trivia with multiple relevant and real-world components.

The SAT Verbal/Writing infuses topics such as:
- Social Welfare
- Political & Current Affairs
- Global Impact & World Leaders

With this, you can see how the students' experiences and awareness about the world and people around them gives them a slight advantage on doing well in this section of the test. I don't know about you, but back in the day, at least when I took the SAT, we would study by just reading our home library dictionary from cover to cover to memorize words and meanings. *HA!* My how times have changed.

Another new age SAT/ACT thing is online and webinar prep courses. I am old school, so my opinion is two-fold. Although I totally get the flexibility of having class at your leisure, we are talking about teenagers, LOL! And two, they can't be trusted nor are they one-size-fits-all. Yes, I know your baby is mature enough to handle their business online; but, for the other 95% I suggest doing a brick-and-mortar physical presence required course.

You would be happy to know that many colleges, universities, churches, and non-profits offer test prep usually around peak season which is October-April.

By now I'm sure you've figured out that all institutions can be just a little persnickety. In you taking time to get to know not only what's required, but expected, your child has "dibs" on the answer sheet to one of the hardest tests they will take in life.

I hope this section made you feel more confident, informed, and prepared to help your student hit the ground running into high school!

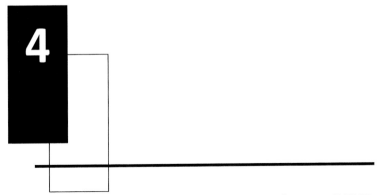

Chapter FOUR

Best Fit vs. Top Ranked

College application season signifies the time of the year when parents all over the country lose their heads trying to figure out if they are on the right track to help get Junior into that dream school.

For some, this day was planned from the minute the doctor confirmed sounds of a viable heartbeat via sonogram. For many, their preschoolers' first birthday gift was a miniature sized future alum tee. But for sooo many others, the train pulled out of the station somewhere between 9th and 12th grade. The harsh reality with this train is many families come into the station unaware that the path to college must be well traveled before stepping foot into the high school years. Because like all things in life, you certainly can't effectively plan for what you don't significantly understand.

As parents, we are very familiar with our child's strengths, as well as their areas of opportunity. However, where we often drop the ball is really putting those into perspective with regard to our child's individuality. Then using their perspectives to help us determine where he/she is best suited or has the aptitude to excel. In relation to academics, the strategy is in allowing those key factors to work in their favor. Think about this, if math or science is your child's weakest link, consider focusing efforts not just on finding every single program with promise to bring them up to par. Spread the focus on continuing to boost their areas of strengths to a level that could possibly supersede their weakness. It is so easy to become consumed in trying to fix the weak areas. However, there is great power in filling that cup until it runneth over in those areas where your child kicks butt.

Balance is a word we often hear that is met with eye rolls. I personally think it's because many of us don't believe that it's possible to obtain balance. Especially in things that society has already done a good job convincing us is supposed to be hard as hell or you must not be doing it right. College ranks really high on that list of things. Parents invest the 12 years of grade school on a mission, not only to get their baby into the BEST College, but with a full ride. Did you know that even if your child can get a full ride to the best school in the world, it won't matter much if it's not the best fit? Why? Because what might be considered the highest ranked college in the country may not represent the items on your child's wish list of things needed to feel comfortable, nor items they value that ultimately play one of the most significant roles in allowing them to flourish academically.

To get a little deeper, many fail to listen intently to what their child vocalizes as the things that matter most to them. Ironically, what Mom and Dad believe to matter most in a college are often the polar opposite of what Cindy Lou wants to matter. Check this out. I conducted a brief survey during a college readiness family workshop. I asked parents and students individually, "What are you looking for in a college?"

The Students:
- Some place safe
- Well known for their major
- Popular sports and activities
- Supportive faculty and staff

Many went on to share why they needed to feel a sense of safety and belonging, along with cultural and social economic status. With this, the students stated that they understood how going off to college would feel a bit weird, but still wanted to try to find a place where they could at least feel some sense of comfort/reliability with peers.

On the other hand, the parents felt the following:

The Parents:

- An inexpensive institution
- Close to home so we can get there within hours
- Top ranked

Of course, practicality kicked in full throttle for parents, they unanimously shouted, "COST!" Every single parent in that room loudly and proudly said tuition/money first, followed by the other items like wanting to be able to get to their child as quickly as possible if they were needed. Ranking was important, but they felt this was because those schools would provide better opportunities for job placement even if they were a bit more expensive on the front end.

Now let's circle back to student response, because after all, what they want matters most, right? The things students feel matter most are super important because these factors can later become the reason many choose to stay or depart within their first year. While I'm sure there are a lot of other reasons not stated, I am certain that whatever the reason, ALL can be uncovered before even stepping foot onto the college campus. There are many ways to dig up information on your prospective institution. Of course the first thing that comes to mind is the admissions brochure. However, there are several other avenues I strongly suggest utilizing.

Here are a few tips/sites to check out:
- *U.S. News and World Report, College or University Section*
  Here you will find institutional rankings and demographic information, along with details on what makes them unique. I like this site as there are also rankings within categories for various things like safety, value, diversity, and size.
- *College student blogs/boards*
  Word press is home of the opinion platforms and blogs. As such there are many insiders right under your nose and who better to tell it like it really is than those who've already walked a mile in those shoes.

Institutional Support First Years

One thing was totally evident to me after getting student feedback about their needs, and that was they must feel safe. Parents were not looking to feel anything but a load taken off their wallets, *ha!* Students, however, are on a quest to feel safe and I believe this is human nature especially during times where we are about to charter seas of the unknown.

The good news is, many institutions have programs just to ensure first year freshman get to the feelings of belonging and comfort they seek. From mandatory seminar classes, transitional programs, cohort style core courses, designated clubs, organization, and hand selected faculty members who embody the level of passion and understanding needed to nurture their needs during this extremely pivotal time. The biggest program taking place now on college campuses is First Year Transitional Studies.

Although you will find variations of this class name like Freshman Orientation, Critical Thinking, or Freshman Reasoning, the same logic applies, a mandatory set of courses identifying the major challenges often faced by students. One instructionally based initiative tailored to address not just the student but, those specific institutional cultures present at the root of each institution of higher learning. At many places, the course is mandatory, earns credit toward graduation, and is a fundamental, logical step to figuring out how to survive and more importantly matriculate the college way.

The course offers built-in subjects and action-based learning on grit, navigating college, goal setting, critical thinking, and time management. The Academic & Student Affairs Staff along with college faculty collaborated on areas of concern often emerging in their respective interactions with students. As a faculty member with the distinct privilege of teaching this course, I can tell you first-hand how much growth and evolution happens during this course. Students always walk in with the attitude of, *I am only taking this class because I have to*, and leave with, *OMG this was such an enlightening experience*.

Why? Because of the way the course runs, it feels like it was made just for them. As the course affords students the ability to share fears, thoughts, and perceptions in an open discussion forum, it totally helps that this is done with peers. The dialogue is transparent, open, and honest leading to the students themselves building relationships and finding supportive accountability partners right before their very eyes; partners who many would not have had the guts to connect with if not forced to do so in a safe, welcoming, warm, and engaging classroom environment. The other part about the curriculum design of the course is many colleges offer various versions. Basically, there could be one for STEM majors, First Generation Learners, Provisionally Accepted, and Transfer Students.

Faculty selection is also handpicked so students are surrounded by those with a desire to help them. With this, your son/daughter has the privilege of working with professors who've volunteered to help them because they can or want to relate. For me, teaching this course was an honor given the fact that I was a First Generation student fresh from a family with extremely limited information about college. I was baptized by fire and was on a mission to save them from the same experience I had. Well, at least prematurely anyway, *ha*! I felt perfect for the role given the fact that I already owned a pair of the shoes the students were currently wearing. With students having an opportunity to take a deep dive into college life in the safe confinements of a class where they could literally get all the preliminary, too-scared-of-what-folks-think-of-me questions, out of their heads, proves to be an amazing way to help them feel comfortable and beyond ready to tackle the unforeseen obstacles of college that lie ahead.

The Best Fit

Riddle me this--in your opinion, what's the best college in the country? Now, why do you feel this institution is the BEST? And what system did you use to this opinion of yours? HA!

Ok, let me tell you a secret...BEST is as BEST thinks. Wait that sounds crazy LOL what I'm trying to say is whatever you deem best for your student, is best! A college might be "Best" or #1 on your list, but you must ask yourself---will this college to meet my child's overall needs.

Now, I want you to tell me what is the best site to find college rankings? *WHOA!* Right? The reality is, there are tons of "Best of" lists, with hundreds of categories. The rankings typically capture key institutional factors that may be of importance to you like:

- Affordability
- Innovation
- Diversity
- Program/Major Offerings
- Technology
- Residential housing accommodations

Let's take this a set further. A college ranked #1 in the area of affordability, can also be ranked #102 for diversity. While you may think, well this is not a big deal, you must consider what your child is looking for in a college. What if a minority student wants to get into an Ivy League and desires a campus culture predominately linked to his heritage. Given this student's desire, would any Ivy League in the United States, check that off his needs list? Ah, nope. Therefore this student would certainly want to seek rankings highlighting diversity. Since attending a college outwardly embraces diversity in the makeup of their population is important.

Also, many students seek a specific type of institution with a strong focus on X, Y, or Z. One that will ultimately mesh well with the type of college student they hope to be. These delineations are of major importance as they can help your family rule an institution OUT or IN as one representing a good fit.

Now that we have discussed #1 ranks, tell me what's the first step in determining the "best" institutional type for your child? Yeah, it's a trick question, the first step is to let them determine and you underwrite the risk. *Ha!*

Parents must understand the importance of peeling back the numbers or better yet, taking one step back to first determine a "must have" list of needs in the place you all will have residence in for at least four years. When writing this list, be sure to add the pros and cons in addition to needs and wants. Each of these should represent just a small piece of your child's level of comfort. While I am certainly not saying comfort is the #1 goal, what I am saying is attending a university where he/she checks off the majority of must haves & needs is essential in landing somewhere along their spectrum of comfort.

What you may not know, educational scholars have determined that more students depart college during their first semester of enrollment than during any other time on the journey. The argument then lies in determining why. Some theorists suggest students just aren't college ready, yet others report departure as a simple correlation to the institutions' lack of resources to support student's sense of belonging academically, financially, or even socially. Now, the bigger question I challenge you to ask yourself is, have you determined the type of institution that will BEST support your child's needs?

Families must be determined to uncover as much information as possible on the front end about the assumed college choice(s) and what's an attractive offer both academically and personally. A student must feel there is potential, in their ability to fit in at the very onset of their deliberation process. This is something I cannot stress to you enough, because an ill-fitted institution can be extremely detrimental to their academic goal of becoming an alum of that institution.

Please lean in closely for a really, real conversation...

Have you thought about the fact that your child's life post high school, may look completely different than the way you envision it. Think about it like this, there are many ways this thang can go:

- Daughter wants to pursue a "Professional Certification/Licensure" instead of a four year college.

- Son decides a "Technical/Trade School" is best for his future career goals.

- Daughter is pressing you to approve her doing a GAP year.

- Son is considering a "Missionary" trip and backpacking through Europe for a few years.

Any of these are great decisions, might I add. I find the challenge for families is the absence of "traditional" college. The other challenge with the above, is this notion that these choices are solely reserved for the average or low academic performer. Be honest parents. You read this list thinking how good of an option these things are for the student you know might not cut the university mustard.

For some reason people think colleges are only filled to capacity with brilliant minds, great test takers, legacy kids, or those with fat wallet parents who paid for a favorable admission decisions. Now, yes I agree there are plenty of smarty pants sitting up at Yale. I can also guarantee that there is an average, around-the-way kid sitting up in there too. The reason that "average" performer got in probably had nothing to do with grades and everything to do with tenacity or determination. I always say, averages matter too. Not just in performance, but simply by the rule of numbers.

In an average, there are highs and there are lows which combined make up the average. In any given admissions profile, there are students present from any one of those groups. Some got in with a high GPA and terrible SAT scores, and others got in with a low GPA, so-so ACT, but a stellar admissions video that blew the committee's mind. The moral of the story is, there is no cookie cutter selection process. If you're thinking about an institution and it fits, go for it!

Lower academic performers are bombarded with folks in their ears whispering, "College is not for everyone." Ironically, this is said, I guess, to make them feel like their grades don't cut the mustard, but it's okay because college was not for them anyway. I hear this notion of how college is not for everyone far too often, and mostly with those who are not the cream of the crop. Transparency moment, I was this kid growing up. So what happened to me, you know with the doctorate degree and everything? Well a few things: tenacity, grit, determination, and self-fulfillment. Each and every one of these words meant that I did what I desired for myself and didn't let my short comings hinder me from setting lofty goals. Very early on I embraced that if I wasn't the smartest, I would for damn sure be the hardest working and most charming, *ha*!

The student who is constantly at the bottom of the barrel must look beyond their limitations, but will only be successful IF they have parents in their corner who also believe in them. What tends to happen is, many students in this "category" do not think beyond their current position. They get overly consumed with what others are doing and what they cannot do, so they fail to conceptualize how to truly make their story work for them.

As parents, it's vital to understand your responsibility in helping your child decide what they personally expect to get out of the grade school experience. The high achiever is typically the grade centered, competitive, 'I will just die if I don't earn an A' type of student or the student who is naturally talented at putting very little effort into making the grade. I must add that in my years of teaching, there is one other category: the student who is 100% driven by life, aspiring to succeed. That student makes the grades as he or she has their eyes on the prize working in overdrive to avoid missteps.

Subsequently, the student with so-so grades may need the additional creative push to just think about college preparedness a wee bit differently. In this manner, the family goal must be targeted in the resourceful nature of simply learning the process before submitting one got darn admissions application. Why? Well because you will want to be very strategic about the other things you do that will dim the light of the impact of grades towards the strength of his/her aptitude to succeed. Failure to complete these steps, often leads to premature decision making that is often responsible for towels being thrown in way too soon or even worse, not trying.

All and all, we know that the parent world is full of those who desire rearing academically successful students allowing them to be productive, self-sufficient, well-rounded citizens. And at the same time options. Those that turn into opportunities leading to becoming degreeD and gainfully employed. Because at the end of the day, your child can go to the #bestcollege in the country; but, if it's not the right fit, it won't matter much.

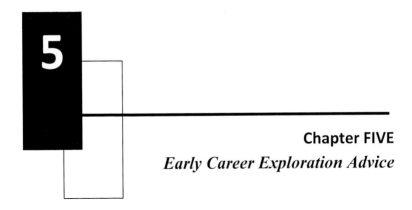

Chapter FIVE

Early Career Exploration Advice

Have you ever heard someone say, "Well, it's never too late?" I personally believe the contrary, "It's never too early," to start checking out future careers that is.

Yup it's never too early to begin exploring the answers to the inevitable question every student will be asked somewhere in their teenage years, or if they're lucky, even sooner. What's that question, you ask? Welp, none other than, "What do you want to be when you grow up?"

Of course many children will just chant off a big, long list of jobs that are trending. Some have surprised me with very clear responses which target just one amazing occupation. As an academic, I was super surprised to find that when I asked this very same question to my freshman students, the response was usually one with minimally researched information. Case in point, one day a student said to me in conversation, "Dr. Okoli, my dream job will hopefully be a psychiatrist." Other than the obvious, job versus career mix up, because being in psychiatry is totally far from a job, what stuck out to me was what was said next. By next let me say this, my immediate response to the students career declaration was, "OMG! I can so connect you with a faculty member equipped to help you look into prep for medical school admission."

The student quickly followed with a deer in headlights look letting me know that she did not know this decision to be a psychiatric doctor required her to attend medical school. She also didn't know that there was a difference between a psychologist and psychiatrist.

I said to her, "Well, the only way you are going to be the wonderful psychiatrist that I know you will be, is if you become a medical doctor." This led us to an in depth conversation about the difference in occupational choices as they relate to the level and tenure of schooling, specifically in the healthcare world.

As you can probably imagine, far too many students proudly declare majors without one ounce of information about where it will possibly lead them in the workforce. Or better yet, whether or not it will be in alignment to what their expectations are. Now, I must admit, one of my biggest pet peeves when advising college students is them having no clue of what is needed to make those dreams happen. A thought without action is just that, a thought. I know parents are not sending their children off to college with just thoughts. A successful college matriculation will take a desire to do what is necessary to put a little sprinkle of action followed by a plan behind it. In this case, the word action followed by plan is an Action Plan.

Nope, not rocket science, and you don't have to have all the answers. But what you do need is to push your child into how to have some conviction in their dreams and enough of it to MOVE on them! Fortunately for them, we live in a world where Google is literally their homeboy. There is no excuse or reason why something as important as future goals could not be researched.

Being around students all the time, I totally get that many just don't understand how research has any darn thing to do with planning. As parents, you know it a little better thanks to the wonderful trials, tribulations, and experiences you've been blessed to encounter doing this thing called life. It is important to communicate how future careers and college majors go together as this very connection helps many students take their future goals to the next level. This will virtually give them the ability to view them from the outside in. The career paths students anticipate pursuing have preset instructions on who, what, when, why, and HOW to get there. Many also have various sets of instructions by the way.

Luckily for your family, I am going to help you out a bit. As for some odd reason many go into overdrive during the final years of high school. Years where they are making a list and checking it twice; yet, bypass one of the most important steps in the game, career exploration. EARLY, very early, exploration is key and I do mean early like preschool early. Well, maybe not that early, but definitely somewhere before middle school.

Ok, I know this may sound a little bit weird, right? Like how the heck can we plan for careers when we can barely get him to pass algebra? What if I told you by making this adjustment to the way you all think, you would be spared a headache and tons of money, honey? In my opinion, this would be like the foundation of the home you're building. The groundwork completed before you start picking out floors, walls, or paint colors.

If you are still not convinced, I bet after reading this chapter you will have a new found perspective. You can thank me later!

Early Career Exploration Tips

What If I told you that children as young as middle school ought to spend time their summers learning about possible careers by shadowing professionals in those fields? Just as academic enrichment camps are a must, early career exploration is, too. Not only to get your child on the right track, but off the wrong one. Early exposure will not only better equip them to choose the best fit college and future major, but have an overall understanding of the "what and how." You know what's required of them in order to make their career dreams truly become a reality.

Whenever I speak careers to high school students I ask the following hypothetical question, "Do you only want a degree or do you also want a career?

As a mom of three, I know all too well the difficulty in juggling school schedules, parent work schedules, extracurricular activities, PTA meetings, volunteering at the school and getting homework done. Only for someone to suggest yet another task during the school year be added to this already hectic routine. My one bit of advice, make the summers educational and fun!

The summer educational piece doesn't have to be just about securing a spot at the best STEM or academic enrichment camp in town (more about that later), but exposing students to the other side of things, careers. I see y'all on that last day of school after the 3:00 bell rings, yelling out an exhilarating sigh of relief followed by the annual run around like a headless chicken building that perfect summer family agenda. You know the one that goes from beautiful vacation, road tripping, and exploration around the city into prestigious camps.   Contrary to what many educational researcher believe about the "summer slide" AKA months kids do whatever and do very little to retain the stuff they learned all year. Many parents do a pretty damn good job to ensure a productive break. But for the sake of this conversation, the one item often over looked: the apprenticeship. In the context of the functional definition, which is simply an introduction/shadowing of a professional.

Now, have you thought about introducing your children to their future employed self? Or signing them up with that local chiropractor to get an inside on the job? If the answer is no, you are not alone. Ironically, many parents don't believe they have the "string pulling" power to snag their child such an opportunity. This makes me laugh, because it's funny how we are comfortable selling fundraiser trinkets, chocolates and Girl Scout cookies to colleagues, church members or even neighbors. Yet, we are fearful of doing the same 30-second elevator pitch to ask the family dentist to consider a summer student visitor. Look, I get it, we all struggle with self-promotion or selling ourselves.

However, we must push them to get things going so that by the time they finish middle school, at least one summer has been spent job shadowing. Then, upon entering high school they know the answers to the following:

- What do I love doing that I am good at?
- What career choices align to my talents?
- What subjects do I earn A's in that can be linked to my future field of study?
- Does my choice require a degree, diploma, certificate or license?
- Will this career require me to attend a career-technical, community or traditional college/university?

So this summer while the kiddos are on break, dust off the old class yearbook and call in a few favors. After all, this is their opportunity to volunteer doing something they might just be doing for the rest of their life.

Three Quick Tips to Thinking College &
Careers

1. Communicate in Careers not Subjects

Let me tell you something, you will be amazed at how differently students respond in a classroom when I speak engineering versus math. Or law versus English, pharmacy versus chemistry, and aeronautics over physics. Those ears and eyes perk up and undivided attention fills the room. Hands go up, over-talking and laughter begins all because now we are speaking their language.

As parents, it is important to listen with an ear to determine how to best connect the classroom to their interests, not how to get them interested in the subjects. I call it reverse academic psychology. The goal is to get commitment and devotion to studying their little hearts for the sake of, "What do I want to be when I grow up?" versus, "Mom and Dad want me to be on the Principal's Honor List."

2. Sign Up For Profession Based Enrichment Programs

Academic enrichment programs usually provide opportunities outside of the typical school schedule to strengthen subject areas like reading, science, and math. However, you also want to make it a point to explore various occupational/professional programs exposing them to careers. Many universities, Fortune 500 Companies, and non-profit organizations offer really good career focused opportunities.

3. Job Shadowing Professionals

Let's face it, most children want nothing to do with their parent's profession. If we are lucky, they will allow us to find a friend or colleague whose career paths they just might want to mirror. With this, you want to bridge those career connections as soon possible. Basically, as soon as they begin to take interest in learning more.

Allow your child to spend time speaking with professionals doing the work, they one day hope to do in the future. With older children, seek job shadowing opportunities so they are exposed to a day in the life of. What we find at the college level is, many students have an idea of their future career in what they see on television shows. Few take it upon themselves to actually research the employment outlook or business environment. Yet, ironically, professionals welcome and are often seriously looking for, students to take under their wings.

The Best Career Exploration Tool

Working with young people at the cusp of making some of the most difficult and life-altering decisions of their lives, I get to play with tons of cool tools.

When talking life-altering, a cool tool is not enough. So after years of advisement and career coaching, I just so happened to stumble upon the Black Card version of Career Tools, The *Occupational Handbook* and *Career One Stop Toolkit*. Both can be found on the U.S Department of Labor website. Although, DOL is traditionally known as the entity to help Americans find employment, these new tools step their game all the way up! The interactive nature will totally get your teenager up and running towards their career goals.

With full transparency, these are not the only tools I introduce to my students; yet, they are by far my favorite. Both meet students where they are, by providing a simple plain language and innovation. With this, many describe the functional use as simply engaging. A user friendly, easy to navigate platform featuring detailed information about professionals doing the work they dream about performing one day.

This DOL Occupational Handbook is a handy guide with occupations grouped into sections then categorized by job titles/descriptions. Very detailed, clearly defined, and providing listings of almost every single career you can think of, followed by detailed information about salary, educational credentials needed, work environment, and again my favorite feature--actual videos. The videos are footage of the professionals in their normal setting doing the day-to-day activities required for the job.

One more awesome feature I know you will appreciate as a parent is an actual employment outlook. Yes, this handbook actually shares the economic outlook of a chosen path and whether or not it will be something promising/sustainable to pursue in the next decade or beyond. Now tell me, can you see how the importance of early exploration? Can't stress this point enough, the importance of getting in the know about what it takes to truly become what you want to be when you grow up prior to even seeking or calling dibs on a favorite university.

All and all, by allowing your student to check out a few of these tools, you can eliminate plowing through tons of inundating career information, or worse the daunting skills-finding conversations where many students just tend to shut down or shy away from. With this, you are truly allowing them to find their way into or stumble upon the "what I want to be when I grow up" versus spoon feeding them all the way there.

The Connection of Strengths to Admissions Applications

Not only is it important to connect grades, interest, strengths, and personality to your child's prospective career choice, it is also important to link those same attributes their future college major. Oddly, many families are unaware of the fact that, career and major must coexist together. Beyond that, students should develop an understanding around late middle/early high school, of how their desired major ultimately impacts college selection. Yes, right up there with best ranked and most affordable, does my major live at that institution.

Contrary to popular belief, college major is a significant portion of the admissions application whether it is fit to the committees' overall acceptance or denial. Think about it, outside of doing your research on whether or not the college of your dreams houses that major, the college of your dreams is trying to determine if you are even worthy of taking a seat in said major. Because, if you can't cut the mustard in high school subject areas, how will you possibly do it in college where the stakes are a tad bit higher? On top of the fact that those subjects will be much more rigorous thus admissions committees often make their initial goal to solve this equation off the rip. Here is a tip:

"The major selected on the admissions applications should be linked academically to what your child's grades have actually proven excellence in."

For the sake of this argument, these subjects will be known as strengths. For example, if your baby says she absolutely loves science and can see a career in it, but her chemistry and biology grades are C's, please be sure she does NOT put on any admissions application that she plans to major in biology or chemistry. Now while this can totally be the end goal, this should not be revealed in the beginning. You may run the risk of someone calling your kid's bluff. I know she has all the "potential" in the world and I totally agree with you; but, remember the point of the admissions screening is to boast, brag, and shine bright like a diamond, NOT to place things that will create doubt in your daughter's ability to handle the academically rigorous nature of said university's CHEM/BIO program. I always enjoy the million dollar question parents ask me after I present this tidbit of shocking info, "So how do we prepare an application that doesn't call our bluff?"

My response shocks them every time. "Create a mash up of their interests, passions, and subjects that they have gotten either an A or B in no matter how they feel about it."

I'll go on to state how this must be. The mash up must be of things that spark their interest enough to be able to engage in an in-depth conversation about them. This may sound weird and people always think it's a pretty super crazy ridiculous claim, because for some reason, they feel it is in some way an inauthentic step in the process. The reality check is, college students are not cemented to the selections or statements they place on their admissions application about their interests or majors. We already know this will change the minute they leave your wings. *Ha!*

Well seriously, this changes given the sheer nature of the exploration process of college. Through coursework, faculty interaction, and peers, their minds may change. Utilize this as leverage to be okay with your child not having the grades to put what she has intentions of majoring in, but can't quite justify yet. Let's stop here while we touch and agree, only to use your child's strengths and extraordinary powers on that admissions application.

For the students who know exactly what they want to do and have the grades to back it up, check this out. Studies show students who do well academically are those engaged in their future in addition to having a much higher rate of completing college within an acceptable time frame. This is due to the fact that they jump right on in, don't change their major, and are focused on obtaining the goal. Other contributing factors noted are:

- Parents are on their butts every step of the grade school journey.
- Early exposure to career exploration via internships or job shadowing.
- Continuous participation in Summer/Academic Enrichment Bridge Programs.

Importance of Online Personality & Career Assessment Tools

How nice would it be to have a tool to help you push your child into acknowledging areas where there are totally opportunities for growth? Or better yet, one helping you to say, "Sorry hun, that's just not your strong suit?" I know it can be hard to tell your eager beaver that although she wants to be a pediatrician, her math grades don't reflect it as the best fit for her.

In addition to the many things noted earlier, there is another variable to get the wheels spinning for families as it relates to career exploration with regard to assessment. According to curriculum maps for the average high school, students will do some type of career assessment. These assessments are wonderful as they help them think beyond cliché things exposing them to the tools needed in the actual thick of the career. However, I must admit I believe we should do a bit more in this area by accompanying the career assessment with more personality driven ones, AKA, Myers-Briggs.

For my college students, this is my go-to very early in the semester. Outside of the fact that it allows students to get to know what they might bring to the career table, it also promotes them getting to know themselves better. I strongly suggest trying 16personalities.com. Work on it at home with your teenagers. It is guaranteed to be an eye-opening, enriching experience for the entire family. The assessment questions are not too complicated which helps everyone answer truthfully. My favorite part is how results are broken down into: relationship, career, and celebrity. This gets the party all the way started. As everyone then gets super giddy about whether or not they have the personality of Oprah or Beyoncé!

By sharing this in the classroom setting, many students laugh or shake their heads saying, "Well I guess I need to rethink my path." Now don't get me wrong. In my delivery of this exercise, the intent is not to get students to change their minds. However, it is done to get them to a comfortable level of conviction. The conviction though, is by design to prevent them from falling into the very dangerous pitfall of the major change cycle. You know the 'every year I'm facing a tough class or a new thing I think I want to do so let me change my major' cycle.

In addition, these assessments can be beneficial for families as they can help you all uncover items objectively that you may not have realized or considered. For example, it takes you out of the big bad helicopter role. As sometimes my husband likes to share with me when dealing with our children's wannabe goals, I can be a dream killer. *HA!* I just say I'm the realist. I don't ever want to provide a false picture of possibilities for my child.

You can believe in your child's abilities, but understand that certain aspects of their personality may provide a slight hindrance to said possibilities. For example, say your teenager says they are interested in being a pharmacist, but you know they do not do well in extremely structured environments and they have also expressed their desire to connect their vibrant personality to a career that allows them to continuously be on the move. Immediately, you recognize that they don't understand the confines of pharmacy in that it is described as a sedentary job. It is also routine, structured, and predictable. One must be precise, great at chemistry and math. You even stated these facts to them and the response ended with, "Mom you never believe in me!" Now, right here, your child uncovering who they are in connection to reviewing the occupational makeup of the pharmacist job will eliminate that entire all-the-way-south conversation.

The other strong notion of exploration is finding out the various layers of certain occupations. Think about those who have many different variations of the role in careers like engineering or nursing. For example, there are many different types of engineers just to name a few:

- Software
- Civil
- Industrial
- Electrical
- Aeronautical
- Mechanical

Due to the fact that each of these has totally different job duties, responsibilities, and possibilities, on top of the fact that the credentials academically, are not the same, the capacity needed to carry out roles and day-to-day operations also vastly different. As such, a student interested in engineering will need to identify first which one they fancy, then manage their expectations, goals, or competencies in addition to a true understanding of what they really want to work on as an engineer. All of this should be done well before they even begin to think about which college to attend.

Again, I cannot stress to you enough how important it is to begin the career exploration journey as early as middle school. I believe starting there is key because at this time in their academic journey they are expected to begin taking ownership and accountability of their academics. In addition, guidance counseling typically begins to dive deeper into career assessments and students' overall understanding of jobs versus careers. On top of this, I believe the level of maturity is beginning to blossom in a manner allowing students to really take this conversation more seriously, since by this time, they have some level of real-world context to bring to the conversation.

Let me add a plug here. In no means do I promote or believe it's effective for parents to push their shoulda/coulda/woulda's onto the agenda. Just be supportive of whatever career your child is considering while helping them to peel back the layers into a realistic or practical option. Make the goal to offer ways to work as a family team, providing deliberate and intentional strategies highlighting the tangibles about their interests.

In this regard, find a way to continuously connect possible family activities, conversations (when applicable), and program participation outside of school into areas they have shared as potential future goals. Another thing I stand by, parents must proceed with caution when they want their children to either follow their path or follow the path less traveled in their family.

The reason being, moving in this direction may add undue stress to your child and impose a level of obligatory responsibility that can backfire. I challenge you to adjust your perspective a bit with this. Many times, the child you raised to be open to attending college or any post-secondary level institution, takes a turn in the opposite direction for a specific reason. That could be self-esteem, academic self-concept, bullying, or lean in on this one...they simply don't feel like what they want to do requires going off to college for four years. Yes, that one happens more often than not.

An approach you can use as a family is find ways to share your perspectives in a manner that displays how college provides more than meets the eye. Think about how many times we have all heard folks say, "Well it is just an expensive piece of paper," or something even worse, "Only smart folks get in." Now imagine you hearing these things as a 14 or even 16-year-old. I find myself having this same conversation with those already admitted into college during their first semester.

What I often share is how, more than anything, college represents a universal nod to the world that says you are able to see a task through to completion. It also provides basic skill sets and transferable skills for life and career connecting students to the world by sharing experiences with people from various cultures and nationalities.

Of course this conversation may lead to questions about how in some instances, one doesn't necessarily need college to be successful. One example students always throw at me is the entrepreneur. Guess what? No matter what, our role as the adult is to be honest and transparent.

Therefore, if you find yourself in a debate with your children, the easiest way to engage in a meaningful dialogue is to ask one thought provoking question: Are you passionate enough about this idea to be fully dependent on your work/product/service paying your bills? What this does is lead them to the fact that while owning a business doesn't require higher education, many would rather do business with someone thoroughly prepared on numerous levels. College matriculation, life experience, and business acumen represents just that.

However, it's also important to understand certain aspects of actual life experiences cannot be simulated in a classroom setting. And in the same breath, there are aspects of the classrooms that cannot be duplicated in the real world/workplace setting. Furthermore, lead with your kid's joy in mind. The best approach is one providing a well-balanced experience towards his/her end goals.

We all know, or have come around to accept, that there will always be two schools of thought. The life university thought, which basically believes work experience trumps school. The other, the college school of thought, commonly referred in households as "the only way". You know the when you turn 18 it's college or military discussion. With this the belief is, one of the only ways to become a success story in life is to attend an institution of higher education.

While both schools of thought are unique in their own way, the decision of what is truly best for your child ultimately depends on what he/she desires to pursue someday. And guess what? Even then there will be no universal/cookie cutter resolution to where they ultimately land in life.

The morale of this story, at the end of the day, when making college decisions in order to understand the "what" am I going to be when I grow up and the "how" am I going to get there, the only universal approach is the one offering some level of strategic planning.

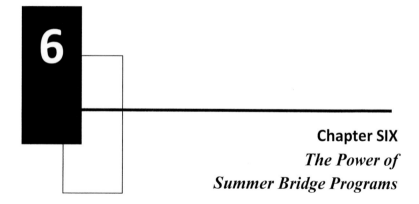

Chapter SIX
The Power of
Summer Bridge Programs

If you have a child in high school, I'm certain you've heard about summer programs. If this doesn't sound familiar, then think about after-school, weekend, or summer programs offered to your child via local universities, non-profit organizations, or even big businesses. The programs typically range from activities linked to things related to college preparation, science, technology, engineering, arts, and mathematics (STEAM), or allied health. Let's take this short list a tad bit further:

- **College Preparation**
  Programs in this category are often available to assist students with the tools, resources, and skills necessary to prepare for college. Opportunities to engage in various majors/ departments, informational sessions on financial aid, admissions strategies, and

summer residencies help prospective students get a feel for college life.

- **Science, Technology, Engineering, Arts, & Math (STEAM)**

  STEAM related programs will provide students with expanded resources to cultivate and develop their talents into an extraordinarily competitive level so they position themselves for recruitment opportunities. Another important aspect is that they often place students in front of those who have been there, done that, both as a student and a professional.

- **Allied Health/Healthcare**

  The allied health category is absolutely one of my favorites given the nature of them taking place at colleges and universities of all shapes and sizes across the country assisting students academically, socially, financially, and occupationally. Academically, students are prepared for graduate/professional school admission by going over good study and test taking skills. One example would be a student with a desire to attend medical school. These programs would assist them with the MCAT (Medial School Admissions Test). Financially, students are typically offered an experience during a few weeks in the summer that provides room/board/stipend. And finally career wise, it shows students not only what the occupation will hold, but the road to getting there from research, internships, lab hours and the overall rigorous nature of upper division science and math courses.

As you can see, there are many types of bridge programs. By simple definition, it is a program seeking to bridge high school students to college level opportunities. The overall goal is to give students the opportunity to engage in a seamless transition from one to the next and without just having goals, but a clear way to accomplish them.

Many parents still believe bridge programs are a one-sided deal that only help students prepare for getting into college. The belief is, programs are only for students already admitted and simply looking for guidance on next steps. However, please take note that this represents only one type of bridge program, although many colleges and universities offer these 4-6 week intensive programs to those students who have recently been admitted. There are many others that focus on pulling in students from the local community in an effort to help them prepare for the road ahead.

Examples of other student programs:

- Disney Dreamer Academy
- NASA Space Camp
- White House Presidential Initiatives
- State Junior Bar Association
- American Medical Association
- Young Scholars (University based) check around your local colleges for various renditions of this program.
- Engineering & Robotics & Future Business Leaders

The names will vary from state to state. However, the moral of the story is, do your research to determine what's available in your neighborhood, college/university, or nonprofits.

In addition to the academic or 'what I want to be when I grow up students', many programs are on a mission to attract those students who are typically not represented (minorities and low social economic status). Like all things, the greatest equalizer is access to resources. It is easy to say, "Oh well, so sorry you didn't know," which happens regularly in poverty stricken neighborhoods. A program could be throwing out all of the information and financial support in the world; but, if the students who truly need the assistance never hear about it, then what do we do? I personally receive emails and phone calls on a regularly basis asking for my help in getting information on assistance/support to students of color.

The Summer Bridge Networking Opportunity

With so many different types of bridge programs, one thing that is for certain, your family has to do the homework before narrowing down what will work for you. Again, first look to state colleges and universities in your backyard as many have a community leg with goals to continuously help students think proactively about the road to college. In addition, state institutions often have a vested interest in keeping talented students home with them. *Ha!*

I have a hole burned in my ear from scholarship and full ride conversations. All parents desire getting that big check written by their "best" college. And while this is an awesome goal to acquire, we really should stop looking at funding for college from such a narrow lens. There are many ways to obtain funding or financial support for your family's educational expenses. Some are direct like a check while others are indirect and, let's just say, these are opportunities. Think about networking. We go out and network or build relationships with folks in positions of power and influence in the event that when we need them, they will feel compelled to come through. Now guess what? Your family must start looking at this college thing in that same manner because networking plus opportunities lead to money.

Let's chat about this a bit more… For starters, you never know who you will run into at these bridge programs. Not only is your child guaranteed a rewarding experience or one leading to college or career leverage, but think about the bonus it will add to their resumes or their college applications. And doesn't everybody want to be a part of such an experience? Think about the faculty members they will work with or even the college counselors they will collaborate with and other students they will share close quarters with for weeks at a time. Now think about this with your networking hat and tell me you don't see the potential funding opportunities in that. The more likeminded, influential folks your baby has a chance to rub elbows with, the better.

When information comes down the pipeline, you want your family to be on the decision makers' mind, even if only to alert you of potential opportunities. What I have found in my professional experience is that the same "type" of families are on the receiving end of all the free stuff. Why? Well that's an easy one, right? Because they are connected to the right folks! Take my advice and start working on ways to get both you and your child in the right circles so they can get connected too.

How to Find College Sponsored Programs

Although there are many different organizations that offer some sort of program for students interested in college, I am a proponent of attending at least one sponsored by a college/ university and preferably with a residential component. Not that there is anything wrong with working with your local non-profit or church, but there are so many enhanced opportunities that can emerge from directly participating with the very colleges we aspire to attend.

The aspect of being able to sleep in dorm rooms, eat in student cafeterias, and sit in lecture halls is irreplaceable in the overall scope of test driving college life. While many do focus on the high academic achiever, there are others who focus on an auxiliary or an athletic experience. It really doesn't matter which type of program your child participates in. The sheer fact that he/she is present and accounted for in a collegiate environment is a huge deal.

At this point, you are probably thinking to yourself, "WOW! How can we locate these programs in our area?" Welp, the answer is simple. Go onto your favorite university website and type, "academic enrichment" or "high school programs" in the search. Most universities offer some version of an YSP/young scholars program typically focused on one of the institutions most notable majors or just STEAM (science, technology, engineering, arts, and math).

Sample High School Student Focused Programs:

Florida State University	Young Scholars (STEM)
Howard University	High School Summer Academy
Texas Women's College	High School Advantage
Bowling Green State Univ.	PICNIS Intellectual Curiosity in Science
New Mexico State	NM Prep Middle & High School Academy (STEM)
UNLV	Pre College Programs
Fisk University	Talented Tenth Leadership Development
William & Mary	Summer Residential Governors School

Pepperdine	Youth Citizenship Seminar
Morgan State University	Summer Academy of Mathematics & Science

Top Notch Non-Profit/Private Organization Programs

The programs on this list are those that target high school students. In addition, many are widely known across educational communities. As my goal is for you to become well-informed, I will start you off with just one, my absolute favorite for college bound minority students interested in pursuing careers in STEM (SMASH.org) – A nationally offered, five-week summer STEM residential program. Your son/daughter would have an opportunity to live in dorms while getting a sneak peek into college-life. Program culminates with an experiential/hand on science learning project.

Dr. Sonya's Golden Nugget

Be sure to check out program listings in your state. A great place to start is at your local college/university, "pre-summer program" or "high school programs" are good keywords to use.

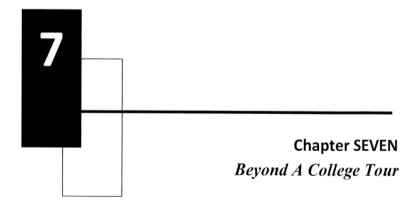

Chapter SEVEN
Beyond A College Tour

The highly anticipated college visit can be one of the scariest parts of the process for our children. I think it is because this marks the time that they must get serious about their future on top of the fact that this is when parents will be holding those decisions to the money test to determine IF they feel what they see will move them to write those good checks, *ha!*

Let's go beyond the obvious college tour stuff. Yes, we are getting a sneak peek of what this place will provide our family for the next three to five years. However, it is even more important that we learn how to look beyond the typical nature of this visit. Everyone knows that if you have time to prepare for a home visit, the authenticity of what's shown could be in question. Ok let me get real here, when someone invites you to their home, they are most certainly going to show you what they want you to see, you know, NOT the things they are not so proud of. In the same breath, you will not be shown the things that may be embarrassing or incriminating.

Think of the college visit in the exact same manner. During this time, when a family is simply window shopping, it is the institution's responsibility to roll out the red carpet. At this juncture they know that if you took the time, effort, energy, and money to visit, then their institution must be a strong contender. As such, the burden of proof is on you...and that ball is also totally in your court. Take it from me, please use this time wisely. I know you will. If you are reading this book then you are most definitely, "the resourceful parent." This type of parent is arguably one of the most vital resources the college bound student can have. Because a father's insight and frugal spirit mixed with a mother's intuition is one hell of a combination.

Where many families miss the mark, is trying to do the college visits on the, "Let's split up and cover more ground," type of affair. I am here to tell you that this arena is absolutely not the place where you want to execute this strategy. Believe you me, I get it. College tours become long, draw out, redundant, and overwhelming. Especially when you are on stop #3 plus.

However, if the family is strategic, the following things should be ironed out up front:

- A list of institutions narrowed down to those 4 or 5 dream schools you plan to visit
- An actual territory plan outlining who/what/when/why/how you will visit them

Keep in mind the optimal visit does not look like the student is visiting all on his/her own. Yes, I know there are tour bus options with the local church or youth community groups offering great prices. However, with the level of information that will be shared on these college visits, the reporting back goes something like this, "I think they said..." That is the last thing you want. Parents, let me make this suggestion, if you don't have the time or finances to travel to multiple institutions, make it a point to schedule and orchestrate college tours as a family to at least your baby's top picks.

Another very key thing I want to warn you of is, when looking at colleges, try to be as joyfully objective as possible. I know it is easy to just check them out and compare them based on your personal experiences. Let me share this tidbit with you, and I promise you this will aid in you having a productive conversation with your baby. Go on the college tours with an open mind and be tight-lipped about your collegiate experience ages ago. Let me tell you why…students clam up or get so annoyed and frustrated with the parents who walk around the college tour either reminiscing about their college experience, or spending the entire time comparing good/bad, or are just unhappy and bad mouthing the college for all the things it doesn't have. I have personally encountered tearful yelling matches between parents and students who are the very definition of what Will Smith said, "Parents just don't understand."

Now here's a recap to spare you from pulling out your hair. Go on at least one visit with your son/daughter. Yes just one. No matter how much they kick, scream, or threaten you, be present at one of the tours. The reason is to show them the line of questioning they should be firing off while they have the undivided attention of the campus representative. Why? Well let me tell you from personal experience on the other side of the desk experience. One thing you never want to be doing, is sitting at your kitchen table listening to your child giving you all the wrong ass information in the world. YES, I cussed just a bit there. Let me tell you if you didn't know before, you will be utterly confused about what the heck he/she is telling you about the place he/she expects you to spend your hard earned dollars. *HA!* So go ahead and synch your calendars, get on the family versions of the tour. Plus, everybody knows there is no better butt kisser than Mama, *ha!*

So go on ahead, sign up for a few tours, have a great time with the professionals, admission officers, professors, even the food services staff. *Ha!* So much that they willingly give you, business cards and welcome your call/email anytime you shoot one off to get the "Real Deal." On top of it all, while in your presence, it sets the tone for how they will work with your student. You never know this could also be the beginning of a beautiful friendship where they start talking to you like this, "Let me share something that most parents don't know..." OKKKAYY! YES! Virtual high-fives, right?

Dr. Sonya's Golden Nugget

Parents who build relationships with college faculty and staff during visits make college processes a little bit more seamless and personable for their child.

The Overall Goal

What would you say if I told you one of the top reasons students depart college, is due to feeling like they have no institutional support? Yes, institutional factors weigh heavily in the reasons students leave, drop out, transfer, or simply don't graduate.

This is shocking to some, because there is an antiquated mindset that the only support a student should need is from their support system. The problem with this statement is that many improperly define "support system." The honest truth is, isn't our support system made up of who the heck ever we say it is OR who ever and whatever we feel is needed to see us through? Obviously for the many students these studies captured, the folks behind the curtains of The University of USA were members of their assumed support system.

With this, the level to which a student feels supported, valued, or even noticed on college campuses matters tremendously to the point where institutions have incorporated prevention programs targeting freshman/first year students with components helping them transition into higher educational settings with minimal preventable challenges.

Commonly referred to as, freshman transition programs, these wonderful programs are in existence to ensure first-year students feel they are more than a number. Additionally, the goal is to form some level of allegiance to their institution that stitches them into the fabric of it. Studies also show how students who feel they are truly engrained in the college community are not only more likely to graduate, but also reach respectable academic marks. This movement has created a major shift in college life, as it makes every single person who may come in contact with students aware of how their interactions can impact a student's experience. From faculty, counselors, staff members to even dining hall and public safety officers, we always had a duty to embrace students making them feel comfortable and valuable. The difference is that now, we are expected to execute a level of ownership and accountability for how our interactions have the power to possibly infiltrate a student's decision making process.

Let's Not Forget Tenacity & Grit

Whenever there is a conversation about being successful, you absolutely cannot water-down the importance of tenacity and grit. I mean, hey, I will bet you $10 that if you Google "characteristics of successful people" right now, you will see one or both of those words used. This is a no-brainer to me because I strongly feel these two powerful things are what separate talented people from hard-working people.

Work with me here. Think about someone you know who is talented with dreams to monetize their gift, but not living out their full potential. Now, think about someone you know who worked like a mad person day in and day out in pursuit of the dream. Now think about what you know about their level of success as it relates to this dream.

One thing I know for sure, the greatest power to separate the good from the great is either an immeasurable amount of grit or tenacity. Let me operationally define the terms.

GRIT: A combination of perseverance and passion for long term goals with no concern for rewards or recognition along the way (Duckworth, 2016).

TENACITY: An unbreakable quality of being so determined that you continue on regardless of challenges or obstacles faced (Okoli, 2019).

One of the best TED Talks I've ever shared with my first-year college students about goals, was by Dr.

Angela Duckworth, *Growth Mindset*. It resonated deeply with them as many felt they weren't the smartest or most talented, but they had a goal, a dream even, that seemed insurmountable. You see, when people hear college, they automatically hear intelligence. With this, folks always assume that when a student doesn't perform well or worse drops out, it is because they weren't smart enough to hang with the intellectuals. When the reality is, it doesn't take being the smartest to finish college; it takes working your ass off for at least four years, through challenges and obstacles that will feel insurmountable.

The point of it all is, support your child as much as you can. Cultivate an environment in your home that pushes hard work, not simply rewards talents. Unfortunately, we still operate in an antiquated educational system where only A's are rewarded. The ironic part for those of us who teach at the college level is, we see the high academic achievers dropping like flies during those first few semesters of college. And the reason being, they don't come with the stamina needed to break through concrete walls or bounce back after receiving a failing grade. Tenacity and grit are skills that must be present in everybody's toolboxes for success.

Please make sure your baby heads off to college with at least one of them in his/her back pack.

Because talent will leave you where grit and tenacity can save you. There are many talented students who did not meet or exceed the expectations imposed on them. For some it was simple, they just gave up. But others they just refused to do embody the relentless ability to bang it out!

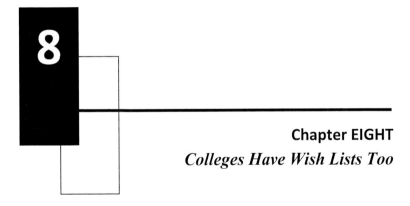

Chapter EIGHT
Colleges Have Wish Lists Too

The college application process can be a BEAST! I often have to laugh and joke with parents to keep them from crying about one thing for certain: how they need to stop throwing money down the toilet applying for every darn college under the sun.

Like all things requiring a selection process, your goal is to highlight what you bring to the table in alignment with what they already told you would be needed for the table. I refer to this as a college conversion rate. Think about what conversion rate means in laymen's terms, outcomes over desired goals based on attempts. By application conversion, how many colleges/universities are you letting your child apply to versus those he/she has an actual chance of getting into? This is not me being "Debbie Downer" it's a serious question, because rejection happens.

The only thing to curtail the likelihood of said rejection is to be very strategic about where you seek approval...right? Think about credit scores. If you have a 550, would you go apply for an AMEX? I mean you could very well be approved; however, the likelihood of that is pretty slim. Now shift gears, and think about this in terms of applying for college.

Let's say your child checked out admissions sites, student blogs, or SAT prep agencies where they all respond pretty consistently to the questions about institutions' standards. Now this is important as the individuals here are familiar given they've applied, had some level of interaction or is in the know with the admission's officer.

On top of this, many share detailed stories, their insight, and the word on the street of a very structured and tedious admissions process. Colleges typically lean toward high GPA, AP coursework, and the upper 10% of graduating classes. But your child has an average GPA, has not taken any AP courses and not in the upper echelon of his/her graduating class.

The million dollar question is---would you apply? I mean, yeah your child could very well get in, but can we agree the likelihood would be fairly low. Again it's important to be reasonable, practical, and strategic.

Dr. Sonya's Golden Nugget

Identify 10 colleges and look deeply into them. Determine their "type" as far as prospective students. What do they seem to desire or even lack from student population? Do you at least meet the admissions standards? And would you say they meet the social and academic needs of your child.

The reason I am suggesting a little check on those admission standards for your desires is because of one of our golden rules. You must have a plan B, discussed further in next chapter. All options should reflect one you can either afford or that's the perfect fit for your needs. So now that you are ready to check it out, here is what you all want to find on the institutions' websites:

- The previous year's freshman class profile

This profile of students provides everything you need to know about how the admissions department weeds out applicants. Below I have outlined the typical information an institution reports:

Freshman Class Profile of Admitted Students Include:

1. Student demographics (hometown/race/gender)
2. SAT/ACT score range
3. Overall number of applicants
4. Average high school GPA
5. Scholarships awarded
6. High school curriculum tracks (Honors/AP/IB)
7. Distinguished high school graduates (Valedictorian/Salutatorian)

8. Interesting applicant facts
9. Intended majors
10. Financial assistance/need

Now, if you're wondering how you can use this information let me help you out a little...Basically this helps you all compare apples/oranges before wasting time or application money. The info is a pretty good indicator of your student's chance of being admitted. Well, comparatively speaking anyway. In this chapter, my goal is to inform you all on how you can use what institutions share publicly, in terms of their needs to your advantage.

All institutions have a wish list. Facts! And no investigative reporting needed as often times it is simply imbedded in their mission or vision statements. If you are lucky, it is shared in some rebranding effort brochure of ways they plan to embark positively into the next generation. When institutions are looking to go in a different direction, they want everyone to know. This helps US because there are often the items they will be very flexible on, so they get what they want on campus swiftly.

Here are a few brochure snippets to describe this:

- *We are seeking to increase our "diversity"...* Code for, we are looking to accept more students of color representing an array of nationalities, ethnicities or national origins. People of color, LGBT, and unconventional religious affiliations need to apply!

- *We have expanded our "athletic department"...* Code for, we are looking to get to all of this NCAA money, thus scholarships for those who play sports are available at an all-time high. Athletes need to apply!

- *We have received "generous endowments from corporate business partnerships"...* Code for, we are looking for majors in all areas of business especially those with a desire to work in corporate fields.

With this information you family should ensure your applications makes it into the applicant pool of the institutions that display an interest in what you have to offer. Not to say that if you don't fit these criteria you shouldn't apply. But, in the event that once you look at their freshman profile you don't see your student's academic performance as a strong fit, but you think he/she meets one of the areas the institution has shared a need for...*BOOM* apply!

Please note the wish lists are very much held in high regard. These items are generally requests that have made their way down the food chain from the very top. With this, understand that admissions advisors will still often take their top priority seat fillers first. Then work backwards to consider other desires.

Alrighty, so can you see where that strategy needs to come in?

The Overlooked Wish List Item, Community Service

As more and more colleges are looking to expand into the 21st century of selecting students, one major component has emerged and that is community service. Students today are thought of much the same as those 70's hippie tree huggers. They want to save the world and "do good" in the neighborhood. Research also supports how more than any other generation of college bound students; this group finds value beyond the dollar bill. That's probably because we have spoiled them by paying all of their darn bills...but I digress. *LOL!* Just kidding. Seriously, I do admire this group and enjoy working with their little bleeding hearts daily. They are super concerned about mankind and changing the injustices that still plague our great nation in spite of what their parents believe. And with this, lies a diamond in the rough: the student with solid grades, good test taking ability, and a heart of gold.

Plus, Highly Selective and Ivy Leagues are growing tired of the run-of-the-mill students who fit the cookie cutter profile and are ditching them for the powerful spirits who desire to make their mark in the world. Listen closely parents, colleges/universities want to see trendsetters, creatives, and the next generation of innovators applying.

For institutions, the trailblazer in the making translates into a well-rounded individual who will have the grit and tenacity to not only graduate, but to make the world a better place; then, yell from the mountain tops how it was because of HARVARD'S belief in them, that they felt empowered to lead the charge. Ha! Do you see what I am getting at here?

Another biggie is community advocacy! These colleges/universities want to see creativity. They are requesting video submissions and letters from charitable organizations and volunteer experiences to accompany that old school application. Make sure your baby signs up to volunteer at a homeless shelter or the Democratic National Convention. The goal is to become an active part of something so remarkable and selfless that it shines brighter than those solid grades and boring 'run-of-the-mill everyone has it like that' stuff. Especially if your baby is one of the many middle road performers where the decision to admit could go either way.

With this, you definitely want to be strategic to get them on some roads less traveled so they stick out like a sore thumb for the right reasons, just like I mentioned earlier when discussing major selection.

How Community Service Can Get Presidential

Applying for college is something families must not only get strategic about, but think outside the traditional boxes. It is sooo easy for parents and family members to guide their college hopefuls along paths that are familiar to them. Many forget how much things can change from year-to-year, let alone decade-to-decade. Once upon a time, the fool-proof formula to getting into the "best" college was simply good grades and high SAT scores.

Now, college is becoming the "automatic" next step after high school. As such, it is essential to grab onto those things that will set you apart from the others. The President's Volunteer Service Award recognizes individuals who have achieved a stellar number of services hours as stipulated here: www.presidentialserviceaward.gov

A high school aged student needs at least 100 hours of service. The beauty of it all, students get the ultimate honor of presidential recognition, personalized certificate, official pin, medallion and congratulatory letter from the sitting president of the United States. Talk about trendsetter, I bet the admissions office won't get flooded with these letter types.

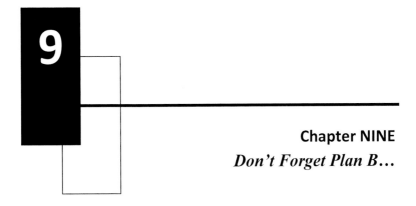

Chapter NINE
Don't Forget Plan B…

Plans are basically nature's way of helping us stay sane in the midst of…hell life. One thing about plans, when they go south, we go bonkers! In this line of work, I have been on the side of bonkers way more than I would have liked to. Then on the side of tears, which I've sat in front of more than I'm comfortable admitting. Hey, now don't you go thinking these tears of joy, denial, or frustration were always from students, as most were from parents. Yes indeed! I've shared a few thousand boxes of Kleenex tissues around the parent den. And let me tell you, the root of most were a result from the dreaded DENIAL letter.

Truthfully, I feel sick during admissions season because I am just as anxious as you all are to find out where WE are headed off to. Yes WE as when yall get in WE get in. HA! For me, nothing is more heartbreaking than watching a student sob because they literally feel like their life is over!

In those very moments, many shared how they are also angry because of an assumed safe bet. Like, I've said before with college admission even when you're exceeding you can still get a "No". "

Just so you know, admissions committees are not predictable committees. Although one of the top questions that I get hit up on in my emails/DM from potential clients is, "Can you get our child into his dream school?" Of course the reply is unfortunately no. Because I, nor anyone in this line of work, can or should even make that type of promise. There is no secret formula or nut to crack on predicting what will be decided. I don't care if your baby is the next Einstein the chips will fall where they may.

One thing I will share with you, admissions professionals look at a student's profile well beyond grades. So while many get hung up on, "How the hell didn't my baby get in having a perfect GPA or SAT score?" Fact is there are many other variables weighed in the overall decision of IF he/she would ultimately be the best student to take that covenant.

If I had to answer the question of what a prospective student needs to have. Or better yet if I had a mind reading capabilities, I would say, the overall goal of the admissions committee is:

1) Does this student have the aptitude to succeed HERE?
2) Will this student fit in here?
3) Will we benefit from an extended relationship with this student?
4) And can we help this student reach their goals?

Let those sink in for a minute...

During their review of your baby scholar's application, they will literally annual physical exam that thang to ensure things line up. I believe parents and students get all in a hissy because they feel they are being judged or compared. While the overall is true, the end game is to determine their fit into the institution's needs or wish list. For example, a student may not be the best academic performer, but there is a connection to how they would add some extrinsic value to the campus or institutional culture overall. Also you need to know that this committee is not filled with Mrs. Doubtfire or Mr. Rogers. These individuals are young, yuppie and post millennial at best. So they want to wowed and not bored. They need best student sprinkled with a dash of personality or pizazz.

Do you see where I am going with this? So don't pull out too many hairs, M'KAY?

Don't Call It A "Give Up"

This college admissions thing is super stressful for adults, so imagine how it must feel for the students in the thick of it all. Many probably feel an overwhelming amount of pressure to make the right decision, let alone the "best" one. Society has a way of categorizing everything, then deducing it down to good or bad; or do this and absolutely don't do that. Wouldn't you agree that going off to college falls into one of those categories, too?

Parents have shared with me that one of the biggest fears they have is that their high school senior will not immediately leave the house to go off to college. Although some stressed college is in the cards, the problem was in the possible decision. Many parents did not feel secure that their child would make a decision to attend college the traditional way.

Some of those nontraditional things shared with me are:

- Desire spring (January) vs. fall (August) admission
- Enroll at community college
- Take a gap year

I'm sure you were nodding your head through the list until I got down to the last one listed, the parent-dreaded gap year. Notice I said "parent" dreaded, *ha!* I think the negative connotation attached to the Gap Year is mainly due to a lack of fully understanding the intent. Hence, like all things we don't understand, we fear it. If at this point you're looking around for your smart phone to Google, "What is the GAP year?" just put that thang right on down…because I got you. Oh, but before I go into the SAT version explanation, let me make start with a little pop culture context.

Thanks to both Malia Obama and Junior from the popular TV show *Blackish*, more high school graduates are strongly considering this option. Let's start with the character on *Blackish,* Junior. He was all set to attend Howard University, Washington D.C. The entire family packed up and headed off with him only to discover that by the time they returned home to California, he was right there waiting like he never left! *Ha!*

Rainbow and Dre, his parents, were furious and confused because he was everything that screams, "Doing the damn thang right!" Top student, high academic achiever, they even followed my advice by going beyond the college tour. For some odd reason, Junior decided he wanted out. Guess what his reason was? In a nutshell, he wanted to find himself. Malia Obama, on the other hand, did a gap year before eventually enrolling in Harvard simply to take a much needed break while exploring and traveling the world.

Now as you can see, there are many reasons students decide to take a gap year, AKA, a short break before the big life change. Now back to Google… Google said it best, a gap year is "an academic year in which a student takes a break from school to travel, work, or volunteer, typically ending high school and before starting college." This is becoming an extremely popular option for rising college students since it offers a much-needed break from the high-stakes environment of academia. For others, it is solely due to their desire to take time to get to know who they are and possibly what they want to do with their lives.

For many, this break comes due to life's challenges such as unforeseen family circumstances, rejection from desired university, financial hardship, or failure to meet mandatory deadlines. Whatever the reason, a gap year can be one of the greatest moments of your life and the answer to a few prayers. In fact, those exercising this option will totally dive into the pool of adultING. During this time, their independence will truly be tested causing a domino effect that positively boosts self-esteem and more than anything else, gets them pumped and ready to knock that college thing right out of the park!

Luckily for you guys, I have the inside scoop on just a few key things, well 10 things to be exact that every student should explore while "gapping" it out. Why? Because I already told you that sweet baby of yours just might be considering this option. As such, I want you to be sure to discuss this as a family. The following items on this list will ensure this decision is well-thought out and PRODUCTIVE!

10 Ways Students Can Be Productive During A Gap Year

1. Travel abroad to explore new cultures and stimulate independence.
2. Volunteer to support a cause with organizations in alignment to your proposed major.
3. Seek shadowing/internship opportunities.
4. Get a full-time job and commit to saving for future educational costs while gaining relevant work experience.
5. Audit/enroll in courses at a local community/technical college.

6. Become resourceful, chat with college advisors, financial aid representatives, and peers already enrolled in college.
7. Learn a new language as many institutions appreciate applicants with diverse skillsets.
8. Build professional relationships and learn the art of networking.
9. Join an international missionary trip or conservation project.
10. Participate in a university bridge program.

All and all, the goal is to make the most out of assumed downtime in an effort to stay productive! The list above is not exhaustive as many other possibilities exist. So, encourage your baby to also dive into their network, connect, and chat with individuals who have walked in similar shoes. Doing so can shed light on other things to consider. As a parent, I understand that you are going to sound like a broken record IF this is the decision saying, "Time is of the essence," and I agree with you 1,000%. Encourage and support your child to make this a time in their life to leverage opportunities and try some things they haven't done before. When the academic year does roll back around, they will totally feel like they haven't missed a beat! Take it from somebody who knows!

Decision to Attend Junior College

Many students, and parents for that matter, find attending a community college is an economical way to save time and money. YES money! Community colleges often offer core courses (first two years of college) at a fraction of the cost. I have seen tuition rates as low as under $100 bucks an hour. The thought process then becomes, *I can attend for a few semesters or long enough to complete my general education/core courses, then transfer to a four year college*. In the higher education world, this is referred to as the 2+2 Model.

The 2+2 basically multiplies advantages that you will appreciate. For starters, money, because the more courses a student can get under their belt, the more money they will save on tuition on the other side. Let me break this down further. A four-year college degree is typically made up of about 60 credit hours/2 complete years of general education courses (history, humanities, social sciences, science, and math). Sooo...if your child takes each of these at a community college, upon enrollment at the University of XYZ, about half of the work is already done. That might just possibly equate to half of the money being saved too!

Other than cost, here are a few top reasons students typically decide to attend a junior college first:

- Allow themselves a "transition" period
- Fear/lack of confidence in their academic ability
- A strategic way to get into a higher tiered institution as a transfer student

One-by-one let me further explain...

Transition Period

Many students feel that despite solid grades or test scores, they need a little more time to handle all of the variables waiting for them as soon as they hit those university doors. This comes either from taking a college course, advice from a guidance counselor or currently enrolled college students. This period may be their time to adjust to the demands, population or academically challenging road ahead. I think this is a wonderful reason due to the fact that unlike high school, which is a controlled environment, college will present new circumstances such as dorm life, student activities, large lecture hall courses, and professors over teachers. Each of these will pose some level of adjustment as it is unlike what they have experienced to date.

Fear & Lack of Confidence

You may believe that just because a student says they are confident in their abilities that they really are...LAUGHS! Let me tell you, as a professor, those who came in from high school with stellar academic records were typically the ones with the greatest fears. And you know why? Because normally they FEEL they have the most to prove. This is understandable, as these students are placed on such a high pedestal constantly being told by anyone, who gets an ear shot of how awesome they rocked high school, how they "expect" them to do exceedingly well in college. This pressure often turns into the fear that they are not going to live up to everyone's expectations. Rather than disappoint, they decide to take the road less expected for them to travel and live out that old saying, "Under promise to over deliver."

The controlled environment they seek is one where they are pretty sure they can rock on out and by the time they transition to that four-year college those balls of nerves once present at the bottom of their tummy's will have subsided.

Strategy Equals Better Options

One thing that may surprise you, there are many 4.0 students denied admission. I don't care what type of college we are talking about. Yes that's right, because it goes back to what I've already shared with you. Just as you should be looking for the best fit, so are the institutions you are applying to. Meeting all the requirements on paper doesn't give you an automatic sure win to getting in. Let me tell you something, I have known several Gates Millennium Scholars, Who's Who, and Governors' Scholars who got slapped with a shocking denial letter. In the same breath, I've known students who got into every college/university except the ones on their top 3 short lists. When this happens, they, and of course their parents, must think fast and strategically about how they will make IT happen.

With this, many have found what we often refer to as the back door into their dream school, otherwise known as transfer admission. Most colleges and universities have transfer admission for students who are entering after completing coursework somewhere else. Typically, there are thresholds to when this can happen followed by GPA requirements. One thing that holds true for many colleges is the fact that transfer admission can be a bit less competitive than entering the exact same institution as a first time freshman. Given this, in the event a student is denied admission to their dream school, they may decide to enroll in a two-year school to beef up whatever they were told they needed to adjust, then re-apply later.

The student delays going off to an institution that they really don't want to go to by instead holding out for the one that stole their heart through, you guessed it, the back door. Just, a word of advice on this one before your baby gets any unconventional ideas. Please check out the institution's website to get the details on what they require from a transfer applicant.

Just Listen To Their Voice

I know, I know, it is hard to listen to a teenager. You know the one who makes so-so decisions and typically not ones you fully approve of. However on this *thang*, trust me, you must. I recently facilitated a parent workshop with a local youth ministry where both students and parents were in the audience. The very first question I posed to the group, "What are you looking for in a college?" Of course this was a test to see who would speak up first. You already know those parents were eager beavers quick on the response draw.

However, when the students received their permission to speak nod from Mom, their responses included the following:
1. Some place I feel safe
2. A college where I see people who look like me

3. A campus that is known to have "some" athletic fun

Now those parents on the other hand, let's get back to their responses.
1. COST!
2. Location
3. Respectable institution

Are you surprised by these responses? If so what is the most alarming response? Well, let me tell you I was knocked off my socks by the students' #1: feeling safe. Not that safety isn't important, because it is, to be totally transparent, I really expected a less sensible response. I probed the a little more to see where this line of thinking came from. Many discussed school shootings and fear of something happening while being away from home. The irony in the connection...check this out, parents' #2 need, location, was that they wanted a college/university close enough so that they could hop in the car and get to quickly in the event that something happened. Parents were very clear in that they would prefer their child to attend an institution in state, but would be okay if it was outside of the state as long as it was within a 6-8 hour drive.

Now back to the students' #1 need, safety. So y'all know I was proud of this response because it automatically proved the underlying theory of this entire book. How well are all of my little tidbits wrapped in "best fit over anything else." Think about it like this, your baby would bypass a college/university that was ranked #1 in the country for their major, in the event that they didn't feel it was a safe place. This says a student is more concerned about best fit for them over anything else. Feeling safe is subjective right? An armed guard on duty may help one student feel safe, whereas a gated campus would work for others. Their level of comfort in safety of that institution will have to be uncovered. While they are on the college tour, please believe they will be asking questions that will help them deduce the level of safety they can expect. That is an amazingly responsible thing, as they for sure need to feel the utmost safety at a place where they will spend four years on average.

Yup, so it proved my theory of the best fit. Often times where we feel a sense of comfort is where we thrive and flourish most. Think about a job where you were an absolute rock star.

That rock star emerged because you felt comfortable on many levels with your leadership, clients, colleagues, or stakeholders. Comfortable to take risks, exceed expectations, and ultimately do whatever you needed to rub elbows with people in order to get that job OVERDONE. The sky was the limit as you felt more than anything else, supported and nurtured. So listen up Mom and Dad, listen to that baby because colleges are not created equally. Your baby has the ultimate power of veto (sorry).

However, the parental role can enhance the likelihood that he/she not only becomes more inclusive, but also values and utilizes your opinions when making the final choice.

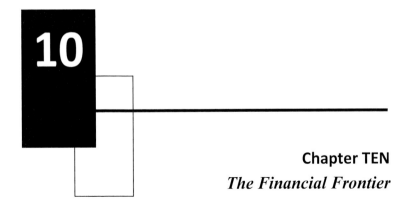

Chapter TEN
The Financial Frontier

By now you are very well acquainted with my background and how I've literally worked up and down every area of the educational ladder from grade school to graduate school. But did you catch the beginning part where I told you I have over SIX-Figures worth of student loan debt?! Totally the size of a monthly mortgage payment, *ha*!

Although not much ruffles my feathers anymore, there is one thing that pulls at my heart strings and that is the financially unprepared family. Nothing is more heart-wrenching than witnessing everyone being over the moon with excitement and eager to decorate dorm rooms and explore the campus when suddenly, a trip to the advising office uncovers just a slight monkey wrench. Immediately, following the look of shock and sheer disappointment, is almost always the sound of whispers saying, "Damn I wished we heard this years ago." And guess what? This was exactly how many parents feel during drop off. Hell, I remember my loved ones sharing a similar sentiment during my infamous college drop off to the school they absolutely could not afford to flip the bill for.

Unfortunately, this is the story for thousands of parents; many are simply unaware of what it takes to be fully *financially* prepared for college. Others even believe there is no way to ever prepare for it. Of course I would argue against that point; as there's always room to prepare for ANY aspect of college. Sure each family's situation is different. Some may have saved paychecks, others created Gerber college/trust funds and a few lucky folks have a wealthy loved one to write those big checks.

Yet it seems as though whenever anyone speaks of college, the very next word often parting their lips is debt. Sadly, I have heard countless individuals who admit they didn't go to, finish, or advance to graduate professional levels simply due to the perceived hefty burden of debt. When I say debt, I am not just speaking of student loans, but general kinds of debt folks borrow from lines of credit, credit cards, consumer finance loans, 401K, savings, or even relatives. Let's face it. This is America, land of opportunity, when ain't none of it free! *Ha!*

Until now, there was a misconception that the only way to pay for college was by earning a full ride, institutionally awarded scholarship. Of course, now we know funding comes in many forms and of various types like grants, stipends, and sponsorships from major foundations. An example, The Gates Millennial Scholarship, a full ride not connected to a college or university president's office. *Ha!*

With all free money, the pot is not limitless. Thus, every student putting their name in the hat won't be the lucky winner, no matter how many A's they rack up or how high that SAT/ACT score happens to be.

Hence, my goal is to get you to see the big picture first and work your way in from there. And this means helping you strategically plan to avoid as much debt as possible. Moral of the story, without fiscal preparation every family runs the risk of incurring an uncomfortable level of debt. *Regardless.*

Let's roll back a bit. In my opinion, the biggest reason parents encounter that financial burden, is due to selecting colleges out of their price ranges. Unfortunately, many feel pressured to send their child off to a college they already know the family is not in a position to afford. Although we all want our child among the best and brightest, we must own up to our reality by instead focusing on "best fit" for our wallet.

Yet some get themselves caught up in the boasting/posting and celebrating of the wonderful, expensive institutions their baby got accepted to. However, what many fail to share is how unsure they are about their ability to write that tuition check come fall semester! Come on now, this is totally counterproductive, right? Let's touch and agree that college is a big-ticket item requiring the same deliberation of home buying—OKAY! Therefore, first things first, avoid a decision of affordability based on your assumed ability to find a way to pay later.

Believe me, I understand---it always seems easy to finance our way into what we desire. But we must not bet our children's future away based on what "might" happen. Believe me, it's best to stick to the foreseeable present when making such a fiscally important decision. One that has the ability to ruin your baby's financial future before it even gets started.

Taking Out Student Loans

This topic is extremely personal to me as I would still be sitting in the ghettos of South Carolina if it weren't for my rich Uncle Sam, AKA the federal student loan program.

As much as folks bash the student loan program, according to Equifax, student loans.gov, and Federal Reserve Bank, over 44 million graduates have racked up an average of $50K in debt with a whopping grand total of a few TRILLION dollars. This has sparked some heavy student loan reform conversations, one of the most popular being an involuntary wage garnishment to 5-10% discretionary income of anyone owing the Department of Education money. Yes this is a radical approach, but many argue that it is needed.

Although I totally understand reform is necessary, especially if we want to see the government continue to help students like our children's children pay for college, I think there is a less gut-wrenching way one that will not overlook disadvantaged families. Or those who just did not plan or did not make enough money to take care of the needs of their family while setting aside college fund money. Absolutely no judgment here, things happen and that's that. Yet if you are one of the families who will need to secure some sort of student loan, it is important to be very modest in borrowing and more importantly take into account the price tag of the institution your child wants to attend.

Outside of tuition, books, room, board, dinning, and other fees can really add up. On average depending on the institutional type those additional items drastically increase that bottom line cost. So again, take all things into consideration before agreeing to allow them to pick the place they fell head over heels in love with.

Ironically, given the volatile nature of the current student loan program there is some uncertainty about the qualifications or if/when they will change. Beyond that we must take this time to shed light on the catastrophic ways in which students have traditionally thought about and used student loans subsequently leading many to neglect to consider the impact it has on our financial futures. And guess what? As always, my goal is to help our future scholars avoid these pitfalls.

In my opinion, the reason our student loan issue is now considered a crisis is partially due to the fact that in the past, it's been discussed with a vacuum approach. The vacuum was sucking up all the information without delineation of specifics or particulars, in turn leaving folks confused, over-whelmed, and with a lack of understanding about where their family fit within the overall context. Thus, any advice given went totally over their heads.

With that said, I would like have this vital discussion "one mo 'gin" but in a way that's helpful to all of us. We will go over extremely useful, practical tips and with context, by grouping in the following manner:

Group 1   Repair, Alum Current Debt
Group 2   Prevent, College Bound
Group 3   Educate & Inform, Future Scholar

Alright, here we go. Make sure you take good notes because I guarantee this right here is going to either save or repair YOU and YOUR child's financial future.

Group 1: Repair
Alum With Current Debt

What if I told you, the government is coming for your hard-earned dollars to pay for your hard-earned education? Would you be ready to fork up the cash and hand over 10% of your paycheck before you even paid your basic living expenses. Notice the second sentence ends with a period not a question mark. No, it isn't grammatically incorrect; I am trying to prove a point. The questions are rhetorical and the point is to be provocative enough to get you to be all ears.

If this represents your current loan standing, and you are the parent with a child you hope is going off to college, then I know you want to do something about that debt. You might not know how or where to start. One thing is for sure, the only way to get a handle on student loan debt, is to actually handle it. Face the facts, then take action about what your options are.

Do You Know How Much Student Debt You Actually Have?

Many Americans have no clue what this number is and assume it is whatever they borrowed up to walking across the graduation stage. How can you have a plan without knowing those raw numbers?

Do you know your loan servicer? At this point everyone should have managed to get all their loans in one place, with one loan servicer. Over the last few years, this was a call to action. IF you don't know where each-and-every one of your loans are, please do a bit of homework to identify the loan servicer so you can begin working with them in the manner you need. Please note, servicers are not created equally with regard to helpful service or the goal of getting you on the right track.

Did You Know There are 14 Different Repayment Plans?

With 14 repayment plans, surely there is one that will fit your budget. So have you made that humble hour(s) long phone call? Better yet, have you checked out the website student loans.gov to review the standard plans available? Many sit back and rule out things based on hearsay or misconceptions based on what used to be. Give the site a whirl. Check out the loan calculators, phone a friend, plan a get-out-of-debt-together party and propose a plan. Then call your lender/servicer to make it happen.

Have You Considered Committing 5% of Your Paycheck?

Set aside at least 5% to a religious schedule of making monthly payments TODAY! Sorry this may mean forgoing that annual summer vacation for a bi-annual one or skimming off luxury items or weekly entertainment outings. According to studentloandebtrelief.com, the most commonly used repayment is the standard repayment option. Ironically, this would be the plan allowing borrowers to pay off debt the quickest. In addition, it should measure the loss you are already in the habit of seeing recovered from your paycheck. Plus, seeing those balances move further and further down each year is motivation to keep going.

BONUS* Do You Know What Your Financial Goals Are?

Are you looking to make a big purchase, buy a home, start a business, invest in real estate or get on the 700+ credit score train? What if I told you the amount of loan debt you carry, NO matter your repayment plan, is factored into creating an accurate depiction of your financial status. Bankrate reports that mortgage guidelines have changed forcing loan officers to count the actual loan balance reported on the credit report to devise the total repayment obligation of a borrower.

To further assist those of you with debt you want to get a handle on before that baby heads off to college, I have created a list of 7 lucky tips. They are totally helpful and will get you on your way to reducing some pretty heavy stress. Each of them is doable, but many require a level of sacrifice not all folks are willing to take. Believe you me, it is hard to change up the routine of your life structure. One thing is for sure, if you feel like your back is against the wall, phone a friend, clutch your pearls and get it to getting to this:

1. Get a second job/side hustle or work overtime
2. Consolidate student loans
3. Sell property
4. Always pay at least interest no matter what
5. Use your tax refund to help with payments
6. Use ANY extra money you come into toward lump sum payments (bonuses + gifts)
7. Change professions to a public service/non-profit organization as the government offers a Public Service Loan Forgiveness. This incentive assists with student loan repayment for those considered public service workers.

Now on to the next group those eager beavers running out of our doors and onto college campuses soon.

Group 2: Prevent
The College Bound Student

How exciting is it to have an almost fully grown adult who is making a decision you support that will hopefully keep them out of your wallets for the next 3-5 years? Nah, not happening! But as a parent I would add scary to the list of emotions because as parents we just want to get things right for our baby.

One thing I caution families on is getting overly wrapped up in the aesthetics of their desired college.

By this I mean, families must understand the goal is NOT getting into the #1 college, BUT #1 best fit college.

For the sake of this argument, fit = academically and financially suitable for the family. Not one or the other, but both. And at this point taking wishful thinking out of the equation. Does this institution align with personal, academic, professional, and financial goals?

I would even go so far as to suggest, we create an entire budget based off the raw tuition numbers just to test out that worst case scenario of coming out of pocket. This way, there is no sticker shock upon getting that financial aid award letter with minimal grants/scholarships. To take you a step further, here are my immediate top three measures students should take:

1 Participate in FREE Dual Enrollment/college credit high school programs

2 Start at community college with the 2+2 transfer option

3 Utilize institutional payment plans and tuition management services

Now let's look at these more intensely.

FREE High School Dual Enrollment

This option saves families tons of money because it's free! It allows students to get high school and college credit at same time by earning either an associate degree or knocking out general education courses. I urge you to pursue with caution as Dual Enrollment programs are NOT created equally with regard to academic rigor. In addition, universities typically only offer those FULL ride scholarships to first time freshman, thus advanced standing earned with racking up these credits could forfeit this.

Community College Transfer 2+2

My personal favorite and one I wish my family pushed me to complete. A two year community college, not technical college, is an excellent first stop option for students. Community college tuition is generally a fraction of university tuition. In addition, it is a great opportunity for the average student to bump up their GPA. The truth is transfer requirements at some institutions are often far less competitive or stressful than they are for first-year freshman. Yet, I believe there is an unsaid stigma attached to the community college, which makes students feel they would be a less desirable applicant. But what If I told you an Ivy League actually mentions---you guessed, it community college transfers? You're welcome, I actually snagged this beauty right off the pages of Princeton University's website:

"Princeton's Transfer program looks for a small group of exceptionally well-prepared students from a range of backgrounds, and we particularly encourage applications from students from low-income backgrounds, community college students, and U.S. military veterans."

Institutional Payment Plan & Tuition Management

This option is probably the least widely known because not all institutions participate. During the financial process, many parents are offered the option of paying tuition over the course of the semester. The problem comes in because this sheet is often shown during the initial phases of admission when the financial aid award letter hasn't yet been solidified...STICKER SHOCK occurs.

However, once the financial aid award letter has been finalized and you know what your child has been awarded in standard federal dollars (grants/loans), before the unsubsidized step, set aside a few days to have a family meeting on this amount (often less than $5K) to see if you can swing the payments. Another option is to look into participation in an actual tuition management system. You will want to ask the university if they participate in one and how your family can get started.

Here's a list of the most widely used Tuition Management Systems:

- ECSI Tuition Payment Plan (TPP)
- FACTS Tuition Management
- Tuition Management Systems (TMS)
- University Accounting Service (UAS)

In addition to student loans and payment plans, parents need to thoroughly review all financial documents provided by the college. You want to make sure anything uploaded on their student portal is accurate. Often, we make baseless assumptions due to limited information, or lack thereof, or missed information on our behalf.

For those who will just have to take some loans for $500 Alex, word to the wise: stop leaving federal dollars on the table. According to student loan debt statistics from the Institute for College Access, Federal Reserve and Equifax Georgia rank in the top 10 for the most student loan debt. Sadly, this includes money left on the table due to being uninformed. As a result of leaving federal dollars on the table, families take out private loans which carry higher interest rates that are non-negotiable, and lack feasible or even practical repayment plans like their federal lending counterparts.

Three was not enough to convey these good resources so hold on, here are a few more:

#4 Make interest ONLY payments while in school

If grandma gives you money or you rack in the dough around Christmas time or even when parents get bonuses and tax refund checks, these are perfect times to knock out that interest, saving you many dollars in the long run.

#5 Do NOT over borrow without a plan

The reality is most families haven't saved or contributed to a 501c and feel this is the only way to secure much needed assistance with tuition. However, be sure to map out your repayment solutions in advance.

#6 Early Career Exploration

It's not about getting you on the right track, but taking you off the wrong one. Many students do not realize their career goals may not require a 4-year university or even the level of education assumed like jobs in the medical or legal fields. This is where resources like Department of Labor's Occupational Handbook or Career One Stop Toolkit come in handy.

#7 BE very deliberate, intentional, and strategic about grades 6-12

Participate in School Choice, Summer Bridge and youth programs at local universities, prestigious private schools or non-profits in your area.

#8 Get a Job in College

For some reason, many think this is an impossible feat to work and be all up in those books at the same darn time.

Now, while it may require some creative time management or sacrifice, in many cases it should be done mainly to cover those extra expenses many over-borrow to cover. Some employers like Target, Verizon, Chic-Fil-A, and Wal-Mart offer tuition assistance, reimbursement, future management, and even ownership programs.

#9 Do NOT Just Take College Prep Coursework

In order to be considered a competitive applicant, many institutions require the completion of academically rigorous coursework. At the high school level, there are many programs including College Prep, Honors, Vocational, Advanced Placement, and International Baccalaureate.

#10 NEVER Withdraw From a Course

You are essentially paying for the class 1.5 times. Complete EVERY course on your schedule. NEVER withdraw from a class even if you think you will not get the desired grade. Being overly concerned with grades can be costly. Be strategic about how you accumulate your GPA and weigh options discerningly.

#11 Complete 15 Credits Per Semester

The completion of 15-18 credit hours per semester can reduce your degree completion timeframe as much as a few semesters. This is due to the fact that 12 credits is needed for timely degree completion; tagging on additional credits gives you a heavier course load and can mean getting done sooner. In addition, many institutions offer tuition discounts as an incentive to do so.

12 Don't Rule Out Ivy or Highly Selective Institutions

MANY elite and Ivy League institutions offer free tuition for low income households with annual incomes below the $100,000 threshold such as Harvard and Brown.

Check them out! Alright here's proof straight from the financial aid page of Brown University: *"Brown's highest need students, coming from families* *with total incomes of less than $60,000 per year and assets less than $100,000, as determined by the Office of Financial Aid, will receive scholarship/grants equal to the amount of tuition, fees, room and meals."*

#13 Borrower Check In!

While you are in college, contact your financial aid officer or better yet your lenders to get an accurate depiction of how much you have borrowed. This is the reality check and inspiration many need. Borrow modestly or seek alternative options before graduating and landing in huge piles of debt!

#14 Participate in Study Abroad & Institutionally Supported Internships

This is like networking 101. You don't know who you will meet. In addition, this is a good way to provide leverage and set yourself away from the pack to ensure an impeccable resume ultimately leading to solid career options when it's time to enter the workforce or graduate school.

#15 Get Involved In Campus Life

College life can be a wonderful thing if balanced appropriately while you join social organizations, volunteer to help faculty or community service, and make connections with faculty and staff.

Also visit your academic and career advisors every semester, not just when it's time to graduate. You could just land on opportunities not yet available to the public.

#16 Enroll in Service-Learning Coursework

Service-learning courses are not just an engaging way to learn material in your major area of study outside of the traditional walls of the classroom, this can also leverage you for future opportunities with those employers or departments.

#17 Take College Work Study Seriously

Many students are familiar with work study; but, far too many fail to take it seriously. Use paychecks, to directly cover college-related expenses. Also, this is one of the best networking opportunities available on campus as in many cases there is direct access to decision makers!

#18 Secure That Major Early!

Do not make a habit of changing majors each time you run into a difficult course.

#19 Think Graduate & Professional School EARLY!

Start your homework on the next steps you should take while you are in high school and early in college. Attend conferences allowing student participation, get involved in poster competitions, get to know the program requirements, and how things work so you have an idea of what you are working towards. This has a way of putting the fire under students to get it done and get on out. The other thing is, if you plan to pursue a career that requires another level of schooling, do not front load your financial student loan picture. Therefore your initial under-graduate college selection must be well thought out.

#20 As Always Begin With The End In Mind!!!!

Last, but certainly not least, the eager beavers in the group just want to get this school stuff straight. Folks always say, it's never too late. Well, Dr. Sonya likes to stress that it is never too early.

Group 3: Educate & Inform
The Future Scholar

For some reason, it always tickles me when I hear someone say, planning for college during the elementary school years, is just DTMin' it (Doing The Most). When the reality is, waiting until senior year of high school to plan, in many cases, is just laughable. In what other big purchase arena, would you feel it was okay to start in the 23rd hour? Like all things you spend a pretty penny on, please take the time to map that thang on out! Now let's ask ourselves, what can grade school parents do now to lessen the financial burden of college? Let me help you with that by hitting my top three in depth and providing you a laundry list of others that are self-explanatory. BUT before I jump into my three top tips, let me begin with my, "Do not pass go or collect $200 dollars tip," The College Savings Plan.

The Scoop on Plan 529!

As a mother of three, my children range from 8-months-old to 8 years. With full transparency, my husband and I just began to personally invest in the College Savings Plan this year. Insert emoji with hands covering face. The irony is that I am all up in this college world, yet just kept putting it off. The other thing is, since I have been employed in our university system for the past 6 years, I just figured my children would use my employee benefits upon my 10 years vested status. Then guess what? My husband and I decided to become entrepreneurs, so that went out of the window. Now, although I talk to families about strategy, I can admit this instrumental step I speak about least of all mainly because I am also finding my footing in the investment world. Then I had my own Oprah *aha*, challenging myself to get resourceful.

By now y'all know this is all about exposure and

sharing knowledge, we are gonna literally do this one together. Plus, I figure for many of you this one might be something you, too, haven't taken seriously until now. Sooo you're welcome in advance. *Ha!*

What is the 529 College Savings Plan

According to the U.S. Securities & Exchange Commissions, the 529 AKA Qualified Tuition Plan is a tax-advantaged savings plan designed to encourage saving for future education costs typically designated by two distinct types, prepaid tuition and educational savings. No matter which state you live in or even if you reside in Washington, D.C., the 529 is available. One thing I can share with you given my many years of service at a state university, some offer university sponsored prepaid tuition plans. You may have heard folks refer to this as tuition freezing. In my state, Georgia Path to College & Merrill Lynch are popular options.

Now here's a quick overview of Prepaid vs. Savings

The *Prepaid Tuition Plan* lets the account owner purchase at participating public or in-state institutions to cover future tuition and mandatory fees at today's tuition rates. One thing to note, as many students desire to live on campus, the student is usually unable to use proceeds to cover future room and board expenses. If you select this plan, be sure you also engage in a personal savings to cover those expenses. Another thing to note, as this is a state sponsored plan, there may be residency requirements for both the future student and account holder. These funds will not be insured/guaranteed by the federal government although many states guarantee, some don't. So do your homework!

The Education Savings Plan is vastly different than the prepaid with regard to flexibility. With this, your investment will cover all tuition, mandatory fees, *plus* room and board. In addition to college/universities out of state, hell virtually anyone (even non-U.S.) accepts this.

Alright now we did our responsible adulting conversation up front. Now let's get into the BIG three strategic tips that I know everyone can commit to.

#1 BE Deliberate, Intentional, & Strategic

Parents must understand "Destination College" is a journey where their child must matriculate with the end in mind each-and-every step of the way. Don't just engage; create partnerships with teachers, principals, and counselors. Expose your children to the fine arts by local museum exhibit visits, current affairs by discussing issues in politics and current affairs ultimately showing them how to become critical thinkers; a critical skill needed to survive college.

#2 Seek Academic Enrichment Programs

Academic enrichment programs offer students the chance to explore their passions while diving deeply into subject areas beyond what can be taught in the typical school curriculum. They also help your child become aware of his/her strengths especially those he/she absolutely ROCKS in! Look into after school programs like Kumon and Sylvan or summer programs at local colleges and universities in your area.

#3 Find Alternative Options to Failing School

Many school districts all offer School Choice programs. Charter school, theme school, Montessori... you name it. Parents often rule themselves out or never investigate those that might be a better fit or closely aligned to their child's academic needs.

4. Read with your children nightly
5. Invest in a family computer at home
6. Take your children to the public library
7. Enter academic contests at school
8. Join clubs and organizations
9. Volunteer occasionally at your child's school

10. Communicate with teachers NOT only when problems arise

Train Up–A Student to Be Financially Savvy About College Choice

One thing covered in the three groups mentioned is the importance of knowing your options then executing a plan. Yet, all of this advice will go down the hill and in big flames if your family selects a college you can't afford. Many parents struggle to have the affordability conversation with their kids. I find that this is due to one reason and one reason only: failure to lead by example. Why do I say this? Well, because when it comes to finances many of our children are accustomed to being told one thing, but shown another. Hey, no finger pointing just facts here. *Ha!*

Don't worry you're not alone in this. As for most parents, one of the greatest fears is not being able to support our children's dreams. Because of this we say, "Oh sweetie we can't afford that," then after they flash those sweet puppy dog eyes, make it miraculously happen. Of course, they can't see the magic that happened behind the curtains. You know how we figuratively broke our neck, got into a bind, or failed to pay a bill to make it happen anyway.

Subsequently, over the course of their lives, they are able to pinpoint examples leading them to believe that matter what, "Mom and Dad will figure it out."

Then one day, out of nowhere, high school springs up on you and college acceptance letters to some of the most amazingly expensive "luxury" schools, all fighting to get yours truly to say "YES" to admission. And your daughter is over the moon with excitement that all of her hard work has finally paid off. Although you are gleaming with proudness, stress and anxiety kick into high gear because there is just no way on God's green earth you all can afford this! But the look on your son's face is priceless and you cannot bear the thought of disappointing him with the news that he can't commit to the institution this fall.

This story is very real and happening at a family kitchen table as we speak. Each year, parents brace themselves entering the doors of our most prominent and elite institutions, on a literal wing and prayer without a clue as to how their child will graduate with a degree in hand. The reality to this somber story is that it is totally avoidable! Yes—hear me loud and clear, you can avoid this crossroad; but not without, you guessed, it a fool-proof strategic plan.

Let me share this, the best thing you can do for your college bound baby is lay down the rules of engagement the moment "I want to go to college" parts their innocent lips. Hear me out here. There will come a time when college talks are introduced at school, with friends or during clubs, etc., and it's fine that during this time they will insert their elaborate "hoop" dreams. Then there will be those times that you guys chat at home, and that Oprah *aha* happens. The *Aha* that convinces your kid that college is very expensive and is no pie-in the sky decision. Here's the speech you need to start practicing before their 1st birthday, *HA!* "I love you and support your dreams, so you can go to any college in the world as long as we are in a position to afford it OR you get a full ride."

Listen! I don't care if that baby is 6-years-old, say it with your chest! *HA!* Then say it every single time you hear the word "college" in your house. I guarantee by the time that you all are sitting at the kitchen table deliberating, it will be drama free and there won't be one application to a school he isn't competitive to receive a full ride to or one that has a price tag out of your budget! #NoAlternativeFactsHere

You see what you are doing here is training your child with, not only your expectations, but those he/she must have for themselves. Don't make the rookie mistake of taking full ownership of the college expenses on the front end. Yes, our children are our responsibility for ever, literally. BUT this journey is a privilege not a right. As such, the responsibility of what it means to have dual-responsibility starts at this very moment in their lives.

Think about how different their restaurant ordering selections are when you say, "Okay honey it's your turn to pay," versus when Dad takes the whole family out and covers the bill. Some would call this reverse psychology but I call it reverse accountability. At the end of the day, college is truly a big-ticket item, one with the possibility to wreck complete havoc on a family's finances. Especially when you have not just one but two, three, or even four children coming up next.

How College Students Can Make "Strategic" Money Moves

Ah, it's over the fat lady has sung. You raised them up in the way in which they should go, and dropped their little butts off to college. The award letter for the first two semesters is promising and you all have accepted an out-of pocket expense the family is comfortable with. Dad gave the, "be responsible" sex talk. Mom came through with the make "good grades talk," oh and, "come home anytime you want to wash" talk. BUT who gave him the make fiscally responsible choices "money talk"?

I am happy to report the college campus days of credit card offers and Sallie Mae private loan options are gone, hopefully never to return. Yet, this sets the stage for a false sense of security by parents that their children now have no way to get themselves into debt. Well, let me ask you this, aren't student loans getting themselves into debt? There are two types of loans financial aid typically award: subsidized and unsubsidized. Only one carries the requirement of parent guarantor. So what happens, if they decide to take an additional course, or online class with increased tuition fees? Well, their balance increases and they are forced to make a way to pay for it.

If you're lucky they will call you first, but don't hold your breath on that one. As what typically happens is they just give the go ahead to increase loans to the max award they can receive. If you are shaking your head in this very moment, you guessed it, now they have accumulated more "avoidable" student loan debt.

Don't get me wrong, many students who get on campus and hit the ground running. They form connections with administration, join student groups and network with upper-classmen to learn the backdoor tricks of the trade. But there are soo many others who float around aimlessly, just doing whatever their friends suggest (dangerous, *LOL*). Or rely on whatever info is available via financial aid offices.

Of course I am not going to let y'all go out like that. Here are a few things your student can do to assist with college expenses:

- *Apply to become a Resident Assistant R/A* Typically students are eligible after completion of the first academic year. In most cases partial tuition discounts or covered living expenses are provided reducing overall cost.
- *Seek Student Employment on campus.* Often confused with work-study yet different. Unlike work-study employment not based on financial need or linked to financial aid eligibility.
- Jobs are from institutional vacancies where non-professional staff needed OR instances where a grant stipulates opportunity for students only.
- *Consider traditional part-time job at the university.* Many state college/university benefits offer partial tuition assistant to employees.
- *Seek volunteer opportunities with departments heavily engaged in research or grant writing.* Upon stellar work, this role may lead to the

justification of a paid worker---then look no further extra money coming through!

These are just a few of the many ways students have landed opportunities to close financial gaps, avoid student loans OH and lessen that burden for mom and dad. I sincerely hope more students accept that financial aid is a "supplemental" resource and do what it takes to think outside the box. Look, keeping it real about the facts doesn't make you a non-believer or even a naysayer. It makes you a smart thinker!

Students must be willing to have a back-up plan for the back-up plan and strategy for the strategy. HA! So in the event things fall short (financially) of what was planned, the family isn't running around scrambling in the 23rd hour to make miracles happen.

Because the reality is, if you all can't make it happen, the alternative is a gutless bottom in the student loan barrel. I want you to know, your baby has options--- push him to get on out here and find them!

The goal here is not to overwhelm you, but to inform you. As someone sitting on the other side of the desk, I realize the challenge is not students or even parents failing to ask questions; but moreso, not knowing the right questions to ask. Guess what—now ya do! As certainly at this point in our journey together you've learned a things you didn't know before. And on top of it all, picked up a few resources and tools you probably never thought about too.

So now, you all have everything you need right in your back pocket. Folks often just don't know, what they don't know...but now you aren't one of those folks!

Nothing Beats What's Been EARNED!

There is just so much drama happening right now in the world of education. Sadly right in our neighborhoods and backdoors. I know these occurrences have a way of making us all feel the system is a tax break rigged for the rich; but let's just continue to earn our rightful seats right next to theirs.

In the biblical sense, we reap what we sow and seeds are planted in "anticipation" of a full harvest. For you, the harvest is that moment when you look your child in their eyes with tears of proudness, as they head off to what will truly be one of the most remarkable experiences of their lives. You anticipated nothing but greatness and expected academic success that would lead to becoming DEGREED & GAINFULLY EMPLOYED.

You had faith in your child and he/she was determined to show up and show out all the way into the halls of their dream college.

I would be remiss not to address the terrible admissions scandal before I leave you with your thoughts. Let me share how much it saddens me because, I've witnessed too many students of color work their butts off to be told their still only HALF as good as their counterparts. Far too many minority students have proven that GRIT pays off, getting accepted into top schools with only half the resources or opportunities.

As an academic with the honor of teaching our nation's best and brightest this burns me to no end. To think that parents, education consultants, athletic coaches, and institutions would go to such lengths is downright disheartening. The rich have been bought their way into elite institutions since the beginning. Ivy League and Highly Selective institutions will always be their playground to getting "Monopoly". Yet, what shakes my core most is the popular belief that the root of evil is money when privilege continues to refute it.

And we all know first-hand many well deserving students who busted their butts for 12 straight long years. Just to see the day where they celebrate EARNNING acceptance to these top institutions. Students are beyond and confused as to why folks would be okay literally selling seats to the highest bidder. Oh and let me not forget the hard working parents. The sacrificed sleeping in for early drives across town. Those who wrote checks on a wing and prayer or gave up weekends for soccer, baseball or tennis tournaments. All in the name of creating futures and options. Given these disturbing accusations hopefully we ordinary folks see, the 9-5 grind of chasing the almighty dollar or corporate career climbing, means absolutely nothing if we are not building a total package "legacy".

Guess what, one thing the rich understand is higher education AND pedigree go hand and hand in the creation of "legacy". Think about it, wealthy families have all the things in the world that money can buy. Their children are born with two backpacks of privilege. One for being WHITE the other for being RICH. These students got Advantage and AMEX swiping at the same damn time. And STILL those parents risked their freedom to ensure that baby obtained a college degree that he/she could be respected with. But even with that our students are still going to get their tickets because nothing beats what's been EARNED!

So shout-out to all the students who have their nose in a book day-in and day-out, grinding and hustling to juggle personal time and study time...KEEP THAT SAME ENERGY! Shout-out to the parents who are out here studying that road to college "Blue Print" like their lives depend on it investing in resources like this book, I salute you!

Although said much earlier in the book, in the end, do not ever forget that the fabric of invaluable college preparation begins when family discussions become college decisions. Because the most academically prepared student, is one with the most well-informed parents cheerleading *beside* them. Now guess who you've become after thumbing through the past ten chapters of this book. *Boom!* Now get on over to that kitchen table and start "Parenting for College".... The only way We're Going Make American College Educated Again, is if *WE* do so as one big happy F-A-M-I-L-Y.

ISSA WRAP!

#ParentingForCollegeBook

About The Author

Dr. Sonya is a Parent Education Coach helping minority families get strategic about college!

Affectionately known as the College Doc, she has 13+ years of professional experience in institutions from Harvard to Devry. With this she worked her way up the higher educational ladder from Financial Aid Counselor to eventually earning the post of Campus Chief Academic Officer & Dean of Academics. Currently between Professor at Beulah Heights University and College Success Instructor with Morehouse College's Elite Summer Program (SMASH) she is a highly-sought after education contributor and speaker.

As a relevant and committed educational leader, she's served as immediate past president of the Georgia Higher Education Alliance, member of the Georgia Women in Higher Education and Institutional lead for the National Association of Colleges & Universities.

Yet on top of all of her accomplishments, wife to Dr. Ogechukwu Okoli, mother to Adaora Kathryn (8), Amara Rose (5) and Arinzechukwu William (8months) are by far the highest ranking items on her "proud" list. For more information about Dr. Sonya please visit drsonyaokoli.com